Tragedy to Triumph

All Bible quotes are from the New International Version unless otherwise indicated. Others abbreviated as follows:

KJV = King James Version

NAS = New American Standard Bible

NKJV = New King James Version

Phillips = J. B. Phillips

TEV = Today's English Version

First published 2006

British Library Cataloguing in Publication Data.
A catalogue record for this book is available from the British Library.

ISBN 1-903921-30-9

Published by
Autumn House,
Alma Park, Grantham, Lincs.

Printed in Thailand

Tragedy to Triumph

God still heals

Richard Daly

Acknowledgements

I should like to thank the many who submitted their testimonies and stories of healing, all with one desire – to encourage others. To those who shared their support through prayers and encouragement during the progression of the book. To Dr Herbert Griffiths for his timely editorial advice and wisdom. To the Stanborough Press editorial team for their vision and commitment in the process of producing this book. To my family, for their love and care in so many ways.

Most of all I give thanks to God. In him lies the power to heal; it is to him that this book is ultimately dedicated.

Richard Daly
(richarddaly@ukonline.co.uk)

Contents

Introduction

It was the summer of 1998, and as I sat at a church conference, listening to various people share their testimonies of healing, the idea of this book was born. The subject of the programme presented was, *'God is Still in the Healing Business'*. I sat enthralled, together with the three thousand attendant audience, as each testimony was shared. Such was the intensity of the testimonies, revealing the anguish and emotional struggles that had been encountered, that no mention was made of the fact that this scheduled programme had gone overtime by more than an hour. The congregation was engrossed.

It made me realise how much interest there really is in hearing the personal accounts of people who have overcome their struggles and who can testify to the power of God in their lives. People are still interested in hearing of true experiences of faith in action. Such true stories have a way of giving us hope to face whatever our personal challenges may be. A hope of the reassurance that God is still able to perform the extra-ordinary within the life of the ordinary. A hope that the God of the Old and New Testaments is still the same God of today, and what he was able to perform during those biblical times he is more than able to perform in our lives today. He is *'the same yesterday and today and for ever'* (Heb. 13:8).

This book, therefore, is dedicated to the awesome power of God, who, in his wisdom, deals with his people in ways that are at times above human understanding but always result in what is best for us.

Each chapter contains personal accounts of people who as a result of prayer have experienced healing in their lives. Such stories are based upon proven evidence where medical examination can confirm that healing has taken place, whether it is in addition to the effects of conventional medicine or over and beyond any prescribed treatment. In all accounts, sincere and genuine prayer by the individual and others is the common theme.

There may be some who will question why such a book contains only healing stories, especially in the light of the many who may feel they have not received healing. The purpose of the book, therefore, is to recognise that healing embraces much more than just the physical; it involves the emotional and mental. It is my intention to highlight personal accounts of these various forms of healing. I have also included accounts where such types of healing never occurred at all, but what transpired was an acceptance of a condition which could also result in perhaps the greatest healing – 'spiritual healing'. Such an experience happened to me.

It was during the eighth month of my nine-month stay as a missionary in the Marshall Islands that I awoke one day with a severe headache and stomach pains. Before I had left my home in England, we were warned during orientation of some of the diseases that could be caught in a tropical climate. As far as possible I had taken all necessary precautions. During the next two days these symptoms got worse, together with jaundice and extreme tiredness, which led to my admission to hospital.

I explained all the symptoms and gave a urine sample. The doctor then took a look at my eyes and confirmed that I had hepatitis. I was told that hepatitis is a highly contagious disease affecting the liver and causing jaundice. The laboratory tests later confirmed hepatitis A. It is an illness that can take between six and nine months from which to recover. I remember my initial response being one of disbelief. As far as I was concerned, God had sent me there as a student missionary to teach English and I was determined to complete the remaining crucial weeks.

By the next day the reality of the illness became apparent as the headaches became more severe; tiredness turned to total exhaustion and constant vomiting. My urine turned brown; eyes yellow; and my already slim frame was losing weight rapidly.

During this time I had to be isolated from the other missionaries while the principal of the school was making the necessary arrangements for me to return to England. During these two days whilst on my own I was able to open the Bible and meditate on the word of God. Beginning with Genesis, I read every account of healing I possibly could. I would meditate on God's word, pausing at the promises of God, specifically noticing the references to healing (See Appendix 1 and 2). I read and reread them, taking note of every word and the promises of answered prayer.

Meanwhile, a married couple who were also missionaries and managed a smaller school at the other end of the island came to our campus. On hearing of my illness they came to visit me. Bob, who was American, had contracted hepatitis in the previous year. He had been ill for six months. Ana, his wife, was from Fiji. Both had by then developed strong immunity to the illness.

They offered to take me to their home. I gladly accepted. During the next two days they prayed ceaselessly. I continued reading, studying and praying. At this point I strongly believed that God would bring about healing. After every prayer session I would go to the mirror to see if my eyes were returning to their normal colour, and I continually checked my urine. I had the confidence that God was going to cure me quickly.

The next day I awoke and, as customary, went to the

mirror. I looked at my eyes. Total amazement! No trace of jaundice. I checked my urine. It was clear! That morning I had a humongous appetite for food; that afternoon I played a round of volleyball and went swimming – no exhaustion, but a resurgence of energy! An illness that should have lasted from six to nine months ended within one week. I knew that this could only be explained as a direct result of answered prayer.

After spending just five days with Bob and Ana I returned to my campus. As a leprosy sufferer to the priest I presented myself to the doctor who had examined me. He marvelled at such a quick recovery. The following day was Monday and I was back in the class teaching.

Although I encountered a physical healing, the spiritual experience I received then was more rewarding. It still remains a source of strength for me to be reminded that the same God can perform such wonders in my life today.

It is my hope that this book will be an inspiration to you as you take comfort in the words of the Psalmist. It is God who ***'forgives all your sins and heals all your diseases, who redeems your life from the pit and crowns you with love and compassion.'*** (Ps. 103:3-4.)

Chapter 1

Anything too hard for the Lord?

***'With man this is impossible,
but with God all things are possible.'***
Matthew 19:26.

Nothing is too hard for the Lord. As Paul declared, *'He is able to do exceedingly abundantly above all that we ask or think' (Eph. 3:20, KJV)*. The conditions of time, place, ability, circumstances and all others that could possibly be named upon which our performance is based have no bearing on God. He is not limited in action or restrained by the conditions that limit man. The only restraint of his power that disables him to act is our lack of faith through prayer. This was evident on a number of occasions from the responses given to Christ's healing miracles.

There are no fewer than five consecutive healing stories in Matthew chapter 9. It was after the healing of two blind men, when Matthew 9:32 describes a possessed, dumb man who was suddenly placed before Jesus. The multitudes closed in keenly, fixed on what Christ would do. The demon was cast out and the dumb man began to speak. The response of the people was divided. While the Pharisees proclaimed that he 'casts out demons by the prince of devils', others exclaimed in wonder and amazement, *'Nothing like this has ever been seen in Israel.' (Matt. 9:33.)*

Today the response to healing through prayer is still divided. There are many who will always doubt the power of God, but to the one who believes, 'prayer is the key in the hand of faith to unlock heaven's storehouse, where are treasured the boundless resources of Omnipotence.'[1] For the believer, prayer becomes the secret of spiritual power. The challenge for us is to listen and become enthralled by the truth, so that whatever difficulty we are faced with we need not fear because God's response will always be, 'Is there anything too hard for me?'

Jo Ann Wray learnt this infallible truth. She shares the events that surrounded her 18-year-old son when he contracted a terminal illness.

'On Tuesday, 3 July 1990, Dr Forrest announced, "Michael has testicular cancer. His left testicle must be removed immediately. Is Thursday or Friday best?"

' "Cancer? Mike has cancer?" The ugly reality tore at me. Mike's face was bloodless. He squeezed my hand as I helplessly patted his. He had waited weeks before he'd told us of the swelling because he'd thought he'd hurt himself on a canoe trip. Cancer never entered our minds, but now it stared us in the face with all its terrors.

'We called friends and family, asking for prayer. Every night in bed my husband Roger and I held each other and cried – and hoped. Maybe the surgery would get it all. Maybe he wouldn't need chemotherapy. Maybe somebody was wrong. But nobody was.

'We needed something to anchor us. Turning to the Bible for comfort, I read Isaiah 58, and the lifeboat we needed surfaced on our sea of fear. The words of verse 8 became a living promise to our family: "Then shall thy light break forth like the morning, and thine health shall spring forth speedily" (KJV). We held on to that promise tightly the whole time Mike battled the cancer.

[1] White, E.G., *Steps to Christ,* Pacific Press, p.94.

'The first surgery went well. Next came a full set of CT scans. The news wasn't good. Mike needed chemotherapy. At the oncologist's office, Dr Vicki Baker sat across from the three of us and explained the treatment for the tumours. "Tumours? We thought the tumour was removed during the surgery." Roger voiced our shock.

'Mike's hands trembled and I heard him gulp hard. I barely contained my desire to scoop him up in a smothering hug.

'Dr Baker gently said, "Mike's cancer has spread to the lymph nodes; several large tumours are in his lower abdomen, and there are over thirty sizeable spots of cancer on his lungs." When we asked his chances of recovery, the answer was softly delivered, "Less than 20 per cent." More was said, but all I heard was "less than 20 per cent." We cried all the way home.

'When we pulled in the driveway of our home, we sat sobbing, as Mike held our hands over the back seat. Later, we learned testicular cancer strikes about one per cent of the adult male population in the United States. Sixty-five per cent of those stricken learn that the cancer has already spread by the time they see their doctors. Those statistics didn't bring any comfort. I kept asking God, "Why Michael? Why does he have this terrible disease?" I didn't get an answer to my questions, but I did sense God's love surround our entire family.

'Mike's first week of chemotherapy started on 16 July at St John's hospital in Tulsa, Oklahoma. He was given three powerful chemo drugs and four blockers daily, and the process took four hours. Roger and I watched the nurses insert the intravenous needle and begin the treatment. Mike slept deeply. We sat at the foot of his bed and prayed as never before.

'The side effects of those drugs were terrifying and seemed even worse than the cancer itself. The list taunted me: loss of hair, lowered resistance to infection, loss of appetite, nausea and vomiting, mouth sores, possible damage to other organs from the drugs, and a real possibility of never being able to father a child owing to total loss of sperm production. Only God could help Mike and us through this.

'The weeks passed. Roger was frustrated and angry. He hates feeling helpless. I agonised, wanting to take the cancer myself, so Mike wouldn't suffer. We managed to maintain a semblance of normal family life. Mike continued working when he could. College was put on hold. The school reserved his scholarships and sent cards filled with prayers and scripture promises.

'Prayer. We were surrounded by prayer. Prayers from friends, from family, from strangers, from different denominations, from Canada, from Mexico, from coast to coast of the United States, and even from Belgium. We felt the serenity and power of those prayers.

'We had ups and downs. Mike would be fine, then boom! The effects of the chemo would crush him. We tried to protect him from all forms of unnecessary strife, like worrying over college preparations. Those could wait. Yet we tried hard to treat him normally. I still yelled at him to clean his room. He and his big sister Amie still had sibling fights. But now we loved more. We hugged more, laughed more. We felt the shortness of life and savoured each moment.

'Slowly, we learned that God's grace is sufficient in every situation. As the news had grown worse, there came a night when I knew I really had to tust God with Mike's life. I'd spent the day weeping on and off over the whole situation. Why Michael? What would I do if he died? I fell to my knees at the foot of the bed, laying my head and arms on the quilt. Tears rained on though I felt dry and dead. I choked out a prayer, "Lord, please help me. Help me." A deep sense of peace embraced me as if God himself held me against his chest. I could almost hear the warm comfort of his heart beat.

'"Lord Jesus," I prayed, "whatever your plans for Mike's life, whatever happens, I trust you." There was no outward change in Mike's condition. Yet a deep inner confidence that we couldn't explain resided in all our hearts.

'Mike's hair fell out in hunks, so he went to get "buzzed", and came home bald, announcing that he was starting the "Jean-Luc-Picard of the Starship-Enterprise-Look". I could handle that. However, weeks later, as he and I sat in the kitchen, talking and laughing, I suddenly realised he had no eyelashes! At birth his lashes were thick and long. Now they were completely gone. I bolted into the bathroom and shut the door behind me. Turning the water on full force, I held a towel over my mouth and sobbed deeply. Right then I realised I could never fully understand what he was enduring to get well. He was my baby, and I couldn't keep this pain from him.

'The second five-day round of chemotherapy came in August. At LaFortune Cancer Centre, new x-rays were taken. Dr Baker put the first set of x-rays on the light board and she turned to us. "Look. Here's the first x-ray on Mike's lungs. See all the spots of cancer?" She pointed then started to cry, the tears sliding down her cheeks. I was sure it was more bad news.

'"What's wrong?" I asked. "No! Nothing's wrong! Look! Here's today's x-ray. All the lung cancer is gone already. This isn't from the chemotherapy!" Her voice was filled with conviction. "This is a miracle! I don't get to see miracles often, but this is one!"

'Mike broke into a big, beautiful grin. Right there and then we praised and thanked God.'

Mike now attends Friends University in Wichita, Kansas. Still totally healed after nine years, he's full of life, and works as a Network Administrator at a local Christian-owned business. His blood tests and CT scans have been totally clear since November 1990.

From this whole traumatic experience, not only was Mike healed, but for Jo Ann it led to a deep spiritual experience. 'Now I understand the work of the Cross of Christ far better than before,' she says.

As a mother, her first reaction to the news of Mike's cancer was to want to take it herself so he wouldn't have to endure it. God did the same thing for us. He looked down from heaven and saw mankind being destroyed by the cancer of sin. His compassion and love for us compelled him to come down from heaven and take on the sin of the whole world in his own body on the cross. There is nothing too hard for God. Nothing.

'Then the word of the Lord came to Jeremiah:
"I am the Lord, the God of all mankind
Is anything too hard for me?"'
Jeremiah 32:26-27

March 1995 became a time of disaster and discouragement for Sue Peel and her husband Earl. Pneumonia ravished Earl's one operative lung. Two other varieties of the disease attacked quickly, along with a diagnosis of active hepatitis C. It was at a time when Earl was in intensive care for two weeks, totally dependent on a ventilator for life, that Sue was to encounter an all-powerful, all-wise God.

'The doctors' reports kept coming like shards of glass. "He has emphysema." "We think he has tumours on his lung." "We've been unable to wean him from the respirator." "He can't live for long on the respirator; the lung's too weak." I was bombarded with decisions I couldn't make. Should we resuscitate? Is he an organ donor? Well-meaning friends offered to help me begin making arrangements. "Overwhelmed" is too weak a word to describe how I felt!

'Doing all I'd been taught, I surrounded Earl and myself with deep Christian praise music. In a commandeered doctors' consulting room near the Intensive Care Unit (ICU), I searched for and spoke out hundreds of promise-filled Scriptures. For innumerable hours, I prayed with all the intensity and strength I could muster. I even got loud and yelled at Satan. Yet Earl continued to atrophy and weaken. With his decline came discouragement and fear. Despair followed, bringing a spiritual fog that made me forget all the miracles I had ever seen, the incredible evidence of Christ in our lives.

'One day, on returning from a quick trip to the house, as I walked laboriously towards the hospital entrance through a rather serene area with several small trees lining it, I was stopped. Just one word was spoken. "Listen." I obeyed. First one little wren chirped, then another gave out a small trill. One by one, a choir of birds joined together in precise and crystal-clear harmony. That song went deeper than all the praise I'd ever heard. I stood listening in silent tears, oblivious to those passing by. In that song I heard, "If I can orchestrate this infinite beauty, I can do what is needed for Earl." I repented from my "works" and simply believed.

'Three days later, Earl was moved to a regular room, minus the ventilator. He walked out of the hospital one week later. Within five weeks of being released, he returned to his job as a long-haul truck driver. Today, over two years later, my husband is still with me, still on the job and still giving glory to the Infinite One.

'Each day the prayer of my heart was, "Father, no matter what I see, feel or think, you are God. If healing comes, you are God. If healing is never manifested, you are God. Your Word is truth and it says that you are Love. As Sovereign Lord, whatever you choose to do in this situation, there can be no other reason or motive for it than love. Open my eyes to understanding, open my heart to accept. My desire is for you to be glorified in me and in this situation. Please reveal to me any steps you would have me perform to participate in your response. Amen." '

God didn't give Earl new lungs. He didn't take away all the other conditions that Earl was diagnosed with. What he did do was bring Earl through that near-death crisis and give him better respiratory health than he had experienced since childhood. A greater vision of who God is led Sue to believe that our disappointments really are God's appointments.

Prayer was never too far away from the lips of Joan Clayton. Upon hearing of the tragic accident of her son Lance, seriously burned in an explosion, she cried,

'Help me, Lord. I pray for strength and strong faith to weather this storm. I believe that you are faithful. I believe that you are with Lance right now, and that you will bring him to total victory! Nothing is too hard for You!'

'I almost fainted when I looked at Lance. The skin on his arms was hanging in strings. His face was horribly blistered, red and swollen. The cotton T-shirt had melted away and only raw, burned skin remained on his chest.

'It was almost more than I could bear, but I felt my faith rising. The thought in my mind was: "God, this isn't too hard for You!"

'Amid the tears and prayers, I began to hear the story of the accident. Lance was filling a tractor with butane gas on my Dad's farm, which was 30 miles from town. A blinding explosion occurred. His face and arms were exposed to the full impact of the explosion. Lance, being on fire, rolled over and over in the dirt. That alone could have caused severe infection. He ran to the tractor, started it up, and amid the pain, anguish and shock, started driving everywhere and nowhere. Lance could hear himself screaming. He drove at breakneck speed, going through pastures and barbed-wire fences. He came upon a large earth tank, filled with water, and stopped the tractor long enough to submerge himself. This provided some relief and prevented further shock. Then he jumped back on the tractor and after a few miles came upon a little country store. The store-owner's car would not start. A man "just so happened" to drive up. He also "just so happened" to be a medic from the Vietnam war. He put Lance in his pickup and raced to town at 100 miles an hour.

'The doctors were calling from the emergency room door. Connie, his wife, and I hurried to the door. "This is Dr Jenn," our family doctor was saying. "He has just recently moved to our town and 'just so happens' to be a burn specialist."

' "He's a mighty lucky boy," Dr Jenn was saying. "He could have been blinded so easily. He could have been burned much more severely. I cannot tell you right now that there will not be scarring, but we can treat him here. I don't even think he will need skin grafts, but we must guard heavily against infection."

'I thought of Lance rolling in the dirt and jumping in a dirt tank that was full of all kinds of germs, but I reaffirmed my stand. I would not waver.

' "God, this isn't too hard for you!"

'At three o'clock on the morning of the third day, my husband and I suddenly awakened from a sound sleep and jumped out of bed. We had to get to the hospital right away. Lance needed us!

'The Lord was leading – leading us into intercessory prayer that was so desperately needed at that hour.

'We arrived at the hospital to find Lance wrestling and agonising in pain. We donned our masks and gowns and began to pray as earnestly as we knew how. After about twenty minutes, all three of us looked up at the same time. There was a calm, a peace, a stillness about the room. Lance was sleeping peacefully in a deep sleep. We could feel and sense the presence of ministering angels. God had answered and the crisis had passed.'

Today, Lance has tall handsome sons of his own. Joan's words of gratitude were, 'I thank God all over again that nothing is too hard for him!'

'"I know that you can do all things;
no plan of yours can be thwarted."'

Job 42:2

Chapter 2

Even unto death

'Even though I walk through the valley of the shadow of death, I will fear no evil, for you are with me; your rod and staff, they comfort me.'

Psalm 23:4

It must never be forgotten that the almighty God rules this world. He is not a God in absentia. His hand is always on the controls of human affairs. Although he does not predestine our future, when evidence seems to predict an expected outcome, it is through prayer that the expected path of the future can be altered. Hezekiah was an example.

The scriptures declare he was sick unto death (2 Kings 20). The prophet Isaiah had already prepared him for the inevitable, by saying in no uncertain terms, ' "You are going to die; you will not recover." ' (verse 1).

Hezekiah could have yielded to his expected fate. However, he turned his face to the wall and prayed, ' "Remember, O Lord, how I have walked before you faithfully and with wholehearted devotion and have done what is good in your eyes." ' And Hezekiah 'wept bitterly' (verses 2, 3).

Prayer has an incredible power to arrest and change the course of events. Speaking to Isaiah, God says, ' "Go back and tell Hezekiah, the leader of my people, 'This is what the

Lord, the God of your father David, says: I have heard your prayer and seen your tears; I will heal you." ' Hezekiah's prayers were answered and he succeeded in obtaining a reversal of God's word and lived.

On Thursday 9 December 1999, the *Daily Mirror* carried a frontpage story entitled 'Miracle'. According to the editor it was to be the most requested story for that tabloid newspaper for the entire year. It was the story of Dr Mary Self who, at the age of 34, was cured of bone cancer after being sent home to die.

Dr Self, a mother of two, said, 'It was the power of prayer.' Her specialist conceded, 'Yes, I'll buy that.'

The story began when Mary was diagnosed with bone cancer in 1983 and underwent an above-knee amputation and chemotherapy. She shared with me the events as they unfolded that would ultimately end as a living testimony to the power of God.

'I sat in the small office, waiting nervously. I had been there twice before, and on both occasions I had received bad news. The last interview had been particularly awful. Mr Grimer, the orthopaedic surgeon, had talked to me about the treatment options available to me for the pelvic lesion I had developed when my bone cancer recurred. The most extreme option had been to extend my amputation site and to remove half of my pelvis – an option which would have left me wheelchair bound and completely incontinent. I honestly told him that I would rather die than live in that condition, but I agreed to consider chemotherapy in combination with radiotherapy. This option would have many unpleasant side effects, but could buy me remission time; they weren't certain how much time. How badly I needed time! I had left that interview incredibly traumatised.

'My cancer had recurred six months prior to that interview, in February 1999, and in that time I had undergone major surgery to remove a secondary tumour from my lung. I had then been subjected to dozens of scans and tests to determine whether the rest of my body was free from any other recurrence. Unfortunately, a bone scan had revealed a large "hot spot" within my pelvic bones. Whereas a secondary in my lung could be removed, and in isolation surgery was considered curative, a secondary within another bone was very bad news. I was told that this time the cancer had won, and my disease was "terminal".

'Shortly after the pelvic lesion had been found, I developed serious symptoms from it. I had suffered from pain in my pelvis for several years, which was now attributed to the secondary; in addition I began to sweat profusely, and developed profound muscle weakness and tiredness, wheezing, and swelling around my eyes and in my mouth. I went to see my oncologist, who advised me, "Do the things you have to do." So I did. I planned my funeral, rewrote my will and sorted out unfinished business.

'In July I became very unwell. There were days when all I was able to do was lie beneath a shady tree and rest. I could not walk upstairs without pausing to rest. I was unable to lift my baby daughter, Bethany. Cooking, washing, shopping were all activities that I could not manage. Richard my husband took time off work in anticipation that I might not survive much longer. My friends began to plan how best to support my family through my demise and the aftermath. Throughout this initial time, two friends, Eleanor and Nigel, especially supported me.

'Up to that point, many people had been praying for me, and I had been to the elders of our church to ask them to pray with me and anoint me with oil in an attempt to bring about healing.

'When I became so ill, I knew that only a miracle could

heal me. I spoke with one of the elders and told him how pessimistic the news appeared. He decided to ask the whole church to pray and fast for one day in an attempt to bring about healing. Other fellowships and churches up and down the country also took part. Over those weeks, it seemed as if there were ten thousand Christians praying for my healing.

'Even though I felt so much better, I knew that the cause of my illness was still there, and from what the doctors knew there was no cure. We also began to pray as a family, several times a day. However, during September my pain became worse every day. One day it was particularly awful and I began to panic. I began to get a new type of pain, which I knew was originating from the nerves in my pelvis. It was unbearable.

'The pain just escalated every hour. Finally, I rang Nigel to ask for his help, and he arranged to admit me to hospital for pain control. I was scared; I thought that this was it. Everybody else thought so too. The first night I was there I needed huge amounts of morphine to get my pain under control. I was receiving so much that I began to hallucinate and have weird and frightening dreams. I did feel at peace though, convinced that God must have decided to release me from sickness. I asked for the elders to come in and see me at the hospital. They came on the Wednesday evening and prayed intensively, anointing me with oil as well.

'On Thursday I was due to have a special MRI scan of my pelvis. This was performed and I waited anxiously for the results. I expected the scan to show that the tumour had increased in size and was spreading throughout my pelvis. Surprisingly, the scan showed that the lesion was not as large as we had expected.

'After a week in hospital, I was transferred to the Bone Tumour Unit in Birmingham. I remained on large doses of painkillers, and my other symptoms were still very unpleasant. A biopsy was taken of my pelvic bones.

'When I arrived home from Birmingham, I contacted as many Christian friends as possible and I asked for them to pray and fast. I knew that it was possible for God to heal me. I also knew that if he didn't choose to do this, then I trusted that he knew best for me. To be honest, at the time I really felt that death would be a release, and I knew where I was going! A week later I had to go back to Birmingham for the results. I also had another CT scan taken. The doctors in Birmingham were very concerned at that point. Their opinion was that I had in my pelvis a secondary tumour that was very advanced, and that any treatment at that stage would be palliative, simply time-prolonging.

'The results of the biopsy had showed normal bone, but they believed that they had biopsied the wrong bit! That was the day when they told me about the awful treatment options available. I went home distraught. Anyone who has seen a loved one go through chemotherapy will understand when I say that I almost felt I would rather have died than go through chemotherapy for the second time.

'I felt very sick on the way home, and when I reached Cardiff I was unable to see a future at all. That night Richard and I prayed a prayer of desperation, for God to lift us out of the pit of despair that we were in. The following day, I awoke feeling stronger. By the end of the day, I realised that I had not had any sweats. I could hardly dare hope that something was improving. The next day was the same, and the next. Then I became aware that my symptoms were easing, and my pain began to decrease.

'On the fourth day the orthopaedic surgeon phoned us, sounding very surprised. He told us that the CT scan had shown a shrinking of the lesion. He cancelled the repeat biopsy that I was supposed to be having and asked me to return for a special bone scan in a few weeks' time. He told us that a lot of discussion was going on about the appearances on the latest CT scan, and that they were considering other diagnoses.

'Despite the general improvement, I did not feel particularly great about things. I had been given so many different pieces of information that I had lost the ability to trust. The most I thought that I could hope for was a tumour that was smaller and more amenable to treatment. I dreaded the possibility of having active treatment, and I spent a lot of time preoccupied with thinking about the side effects of treatment, contemplating hair loss, sickness, undergoing an early menopause and the very real possibility of dying from major complications. It seemed too much to cope with. I also knew about the permanent side effects of radiotherapy, and the thought of chronic illness filled me with misery.

'"Haven't I been through enough, God?" I asked. "It just doesn't seem fair that I have to go through more."

'In my anger I turned away from relying on God, and tried to look for other ways. I was desperate for a way out. I started to drink a lot of alcohol, and I made up a little fantasy world, where I could escape. It was pretty easy to do that, as I was still on my strong painkillers. My mood was very low, and my relationships began to suffer; I felt angry and resentful a lot of the time. Spiritually, my peace with the Lord was also being eroded. One night I hit a bit of an all-time low. I went out, got horribly drunk and did a lot of really destructive things. I just wanted to shout and scream and stamp my feet; I was so fed up with the whole business of being ill, having tests and living with uncertainty and threat.

'The following day I awoke with a bad hangover and a feeling of utter despair. I opened my Bible and read through the words of Psalm 91, a psalm I always read when situations seem hopeless.

'"He who dwells in the shelter of the Most High will rest in the shadow of the Almighty," I read. And at the end, "I will deliver him and honour him. With long life will I satisfy him and show him my salvation."

'I realised from these words that I would find rest only if I dwelt in his shelter. I needed to put the stupid things I was doing behind me, and turn back to trusting God. I repented of drinking heavily and wrecking my relationships with others, and I turned back to him, asking him to help me.

'The following week I went to church and heard a preacher from Florida. He shared accounts with us of people whom he had seen cured of various cancers and terminal illnesses after putting their trust and faith in God. They had been healed in a time of spiritual revival at their churches, when they had seen the Spirit of God sweep through their city and change lives dramatically. He told us that we had to put our lives right before we could expect to see God's Spirit move in power. At the end of the service I went forward and asked God to cleanse and change my heart from anger to acceptance, and then I went and asked for prayer and anointing for healing. I did not feel anything incredible, just a deep inner peace and certainty that I was in God's hands.

'On the Tuesday I met once again with the elders from my own church and once again received prayer and anointing for healing. I was convinced that God was at work in my life. By this time it was three weeks since I had experienced any symptoms or severe pain. I had cut down my medication from being on ten different drugs, including three types of strong painkillers, to just one painkiller and the anti-depressant that I had been on for several years.

'After the session of prayer, a good friend of mine asked me if there was anything that I needed to put right in my life; she knew that I had a vital bone scan the following day. There were two things that I felt were wrong in my life, one of which involved making an apology to one of my friends. I put the things right as best I could. I knew that the day of the scan was a really important step in my Christian journey. Many people had committed themselves to praying and fasting on the day of the scan, and I believed that I had done everything I needed to. My life was clean, I had faith that I could be healed and I had done as the word of God told me.

'Eleanor, one of my Christian friends, and I arrived in Birmingham. I can honestly say that it was the only time that I had felt completely unconcerned about an investigation. I received an injection of a radioactive isotope, and it was arranged for me to come back to have my bone scans taken several hours later. Normally at that stage I would have felt ill, tired and anxious, but Eleanor and I just had a great time; we laughed and laughed for two hours. I went back for the bone scan, which involved lying still under a special camera. I knew that things were looking good when the radiographer asked me where the lesion was meant to be! We headed back to see the doctors at the Bone Tumour Unit, having sneaked a little look at the scan pictures. I'm no expert at reading scans, but I certainly couldn't see much.

'Ellie and I reassured each other all the way back. "Maybe there is something that I have missed. I don't want to get my hopes up," I told Ellie. Then we found ourselves sitting back in the poky office where this story began.

'The doctors entered with big smiles on their faces. They looked at me in disbelief, and sat down. The room was silent and I waited for Mr Grimer to begin.

' "Have you seen these scans?" he asked. Not wishing to be caught sneaking a look at my films, I hedged my bets.

"Mmm, yes, but only a quick glance."

' "What do you think?" he asked. I felt a little like a medical student again. "Well, I'm not too great on scans, but I couldn't see much."

' "There is *nothing* on them," Mr Grimer told me with a huge grin on his face. "Nothing! The lesion has gone completely."

'There was silence as I took this in. My heart rate increased, and I felt a huge wave of peace and warmth wash over me.

' "We are totally unable to explain these results," he continued. "We just cannot understand what has happened. Can you?"

'Ellie and I had chatted over how to react to this question. "Well, I am a Christian, and I believe that God can heal people. We have been praying for healing." I hesitated slightly, not wanting to be laughed out of the room. "I think that it is a miracle."

'There was another silence as Mr Grimer, one of the world authorities on bone tumours, looked straight at me and very definitely said, "Yes. I'll buy that."

'Both of these eminent doctors just kept on looking at me, shaking their heads in disbelief.

' "You are a new woman," Dr Spooner, the oncologist, said. "Have you had any of the other symptoms?"

' "No, they all stopped about three weeks ago." I explained. "And the pain has gradually decreased too. I feel great, really strong and well."

' "Well, you look great," he agreed. "Your whole appearance is different; your posture is straight; your eyes are bright. You look completely different from a few months ago. Basically, we have done nothing to you and you have recovered from what we had all decided was a terminal illness." As he finished, he could not stop smiling.

'"Could you have been wrong about the diagnosis?" I asked, knowing that there had been some discussion about alternatives.

'"No, Mary," Mr Grimer told me. "We thought about other things but, basically, nothing else fitted. When you were referred here, everybody was extremely concerned about you. Professor Mason and Dr Schmidt thought, given the severity of your symptoms, the level of pain and all the previous results, that you were dying. To be honest we agreed with them."

'"We thought that we would come here today and see a very different picture," continued Dr Spooner, "We expected to see a very ill lady, not someone who is a picture of health. We are stunned."

'"Nothing explains the differences in the two bone scans," admitted Mr Grimer. "Last time, you had very active lesion that was typical of a bone secondary; this time there is nothing."

'"It couldn't have been a fracture?" I asked, desperate to be convinced.

'"No!" Mr Grimer shook his head for emphasis. "A fracture would not heal like this, so quickly and completely, nor would it explain the other symptoms disappearing or the pain resolving. You are in a category of your own, completely unexplainable. Secondaries don't do this. Nothing does this!"

'"How about my own category being one of miracles?" I asked.

'"If you like," he agreed. "I guess the amazing thing is that you are better, and we don't need to see you again!

'"Your prognosis has just gone from being terminal, to having had a curative procedure for a solitary lung secondary, which is now history. We shall, of course, keep an eye on you in the future."

'Then they shook my hand and walked out, still looking completely dazed.

'Ellie and I flew home that night and sang all the way. We kept looking at each other and asking if it was all true, and then we just laughed. Although everybody had prayed for healing, now that it had happened in such an amazing way it was hard to believe. That night I slept my first night without dreaming about cancer. I woke up with a song of praise in my heart, and I am still singing. It feels a bit like I had been sitting on death row, and someone had just opened those heavy doors and let me out.

'I don't know what God plans in the future for me. Maybe I will never get sick again, and live to be ninety. Maybe God has healed me for a time, until I've completed his purposes in my life. I don't know, but it doesn't matter. I have learnt that I can trust him "even unto death." '

'For this is God, our God for ever and ever;
He will be our guide even to death.'
Psalm 48:14, KJV

Chapter 3

Linked by prayer

'The Lord is near to all who call on him,
to all who call on him in truth.
He fulfils the desires of those who fear him;
he hears their cry and saves them.'

Psalm 145:18-19

Faith and prayer can be described as two channels which inseperably flow into one.

The possibilities of prayer are the possibilities of faith. Prayer combined with faith is what moves the hand of God. It unlocks heaven's storehouse of undiminished power from God. It moves the hand of the One who moves the world. Prayer is the dominant link between man and God where his healing power is displayed.

We learn a valuable lesson of faith and prayer through the miraculous healing of the centurion's servant. The simplicity and strength of the faith of the Roman officer are remarkable, for he believed that it was not necessary for the Lord to go directly to his house in order to have his request granted, but to 'just say the word, and my servant will be healed' (Matt. 8:8). Jesus put his mark upon this man's faith by saying, 'I have not found anyone in Israel with such great faith' (v. 10). This man's prayer was the expression of his strong faith, and such faith brought the answer promptly.

We get the same invaluable lesson in the case of the Syrophoenician woman who went to Jesus on behalf of her stricken daughter, making her daughter's case her own by pleading, 'Lord, help me' (Matt. 15:25). A wonderful example of intercessory prayer. Jesus seemingly held her off for a while, but at last yielded and put his seal of approval upon her by saying, ' "Woman, you have great faith!" '(v. 28).

Today it seems the utmost possibilities of prayer have rarely been realised. The promises of God are so great that it almost staggers our faith and causes us to hesitate with astonishment. His promise to answer, to do and to give 'all things,' 'any thing,' 'whatsoever,' and 'all things whatsoever,' is so large, so great, so exceedingly broad, that we stand back in amazement and give ourselves over to questioning and doubt. Let us ever keep in mind, and never for one moment allow ourselves to doubt, the statement that God means what he says and says what he means.

God's promises are his own word. Today by faith we can draw on his healing power, as did the prayer warriors of the Bible. The Scriptures are filled with precious promises where God invokes his people to pray, believing. (See Appendix 1)

Robert Diacheysn Jnr was one who sought to claim these promises. God answered his prayer in healing his 1-year-old son who had had to endure the sufferings of a neuromuscular disease. Prayers came in various ways, including the channel of the Internet. Here he journals the events that took place:

'Sunday am: It had been a week of sleepless nights, struggling with our 1-year-old son Dakota. As he cried out in pain, my wife Sharon and I decided to take him to the hospital. He had, at this point, lost the use of his legs.

'Sunday pm: After a long day of blood tests, prodding and probing, the doctor decides to admit Dakota for further testing. Diagnosis: unknown.

'Monday am: The doctor informs us that Dakota may have contracted any one of a number of neuromuscular diseases, some of them considerably more serious than others. We are told he must undergo an EEG, an MRI, and a lumbar puncture. We are warned that there is "cause for concern". Diagnosis: still unknown.

'Monday pm: Upon arriving home, I am greeted with a barrage of phone messages, offering sincere concern and prayers from dear friends. I go on the Internet to send messages to a few friends, explaining why I will not be available to fulfil my obligations to them this week. "Coincidentally", I bump into a dear old friend from New Jersey. I tell him the situation and he promises to spread the word to our friends up North, so that they can pray. Suddenly, I remember a close friend here in Florida who has a daily devotional that reaches thousands. I fire off a quick email, asking for prayer.

'Tuesday noon: Dakota is diagnosed with Guillain-Barre Syndrome: a rare neuromuscular disorder in which the immune system attacks the protein in healthy cells, resulting in temporary paralysis. We are relieved to have a diagnosis and to know that this syndrome is never fatal; it does, however, call for constant monitoring of the heart and lungs and can last for weeks, months, or even years!

'Tuesday pm: Upon arriving home, I am bombarded with phone calls and emails from praying Christians around the world! Everyone seemed to be praying for our baby's healing! I send an update and return countless local calls from well-wishers asking, "How can we help?" Sharon and Dakota are inundated with hospital visits, gifts, meals, love, and PRAYER, PRAYER, PRAYER!

'Wednesday: Dakota's condition takes a dramatic turn –

upward! For some reason he is sitting up, kicking his legs, eating and laughing. Coincidence? Or is God send ing an "Instant Message" of his own?

'Thursday and Friday: Dakota's condition continues to improve remarkably. Our family continues to be blessed by the love and care and constant intercession of God's children everywhere.

'Saturday pm: Dakota comes home! The doctor is pleased and amazed at his rapid recovery. He tells us, "He may be completely cured in as little as a week or two!" I go on the computer once more, this time to report the "good news": God still hears and answers our prayers! He is a God of Miracles!

'Six months have passed since this time and Dakota is now completely healed, walking and showing no sign of ever having been infected! We continue to PRAISE the Lord who heals!'

In this age of fast-paced, cyberspace technology, we can communicate faster than ever before. God can use something like the Internet to carry needs, answers, and messages of hope around the globe in just seconds. Yet he knows the desires of our hearts before the words ever leave our lips. He inhabits the prayers of his people. We can be thankful that we are all 'connected' to a God who never goes 'offline.'

'Before they call I will answer;
while they are still speaking I will hear.'

Isaiah 65:24

Another method of prayer is through the biblically-prescribed means of the anointing service, as described by James. *'Is any one of you sick? He should call the elders of the church to pray over him and anoint him with oil in the name of the Lord. And the prayer offered in faith will make the sick person well; the Lord will raise him up.' James 5:14-16.*

Pastor Ken Clothier shares the story of how, while he was ministering in the city of York, an anointing service for one of his church members brought results that baffled the medical staff.

'The city of York in northern England is probably the most fascinating of all the cities where I have been privileged to work.

'On one of my home visits I was puzzled to find Charles Barker sitting on a chair with his trousers rolled up his legs. His feet rested in a bowl of warm water, and his legs appeared very swollen.

'I quickly discovered that he had gangrene and was trying to encourage the circulation of the blood to his lower limbs. His condition worsened over the next few weeks and he was admitted to hospital.

'The nurse in charge of his ward brought him the fearful news that he would need to have at least one of his legs amputated. With his customary smiling face he turned to the nurse and said, "No, that will not be necessary." Here was a qualified nurse, in co-operation with the doctor, understanding the gravity of the situation, presenting to her patient the only life-saving cure she knew, and the patient replied by saying, "No, that will not be necessary." Charles invited the elder of the church and me to the hospital to conduct a service of anointing.

'The expression on the nurse's face when we arrived will live with me forever. She looked at us as though we belonged to another planet. It became obvious that our beloved brother had made all the necessary arrangements for our arrival, because when I asked the nurse if we could use a private room for anointing she simply looked at us incredulously, pointed in the direction of an empty room, and appeared utterly speechless.

'This was an awesome moment which needed tremendous faith, and I felt totally unworthy to lead in the service that was to follow. The realisation struck me forcefully that if any of us were harbouring a single sin, however small, then God would not be able to help us. We searched our hearts. We read. We prayed. The anointing followed, but nothing of a miraculous nature took place. After a while the elder and I left the hospital and made our way home.

'A short time later Charles was discharged from hospital. The fact was that although there was no apparent instant and complete cure, the blood circulation in his legs had gradually begun to return to normal. He was back on his bike, spreading Gospel literature through the villages where he lived, just as had been his custom for many years. One year later our Charles Baker returned to the hospital for a check-up. A new doctor read his notes and said, "Mr Barker, if I had been here a year ago, I would have certainly removed your leg." Does God answer prayer?'

'You will pray to him, and he will hear you.'
Job 22:27

Brendalyn Martin received healing from diabetes as a result of personal, persevering prayer. She was diagnosed with diabetes and hospitalised with a blood sugar of 1293 on 24 May 1999. She was severely dehydrated and the doctors and nurses in the Intensive Care Unit said that with a blood sugar that high she ought to have been in a coma or even dead. However, Brendalyn knew that through all this God's hands were upon her. She continues her story:

'Before I was hospitalised, when I knew something was wrong but did not know what, I continually prayed and stood on God's Word that *"by his stripes we are healed."*

'I was released from the hospital a week later with my blood sugars still at the 200 mark and taking 74 units of insulin a day. I continued to pray that I would not need the insulin, especially since I have a deep aversion to needles. Within a week it was down to 100 and I had problems keeping it up. Over the next three weeks, they lowered the dosage, and a month after leaving the hospital I was taken off insulin and placed on one Glyburide tablet a day, the lowest dose.

'I continued to pray that I would not need any medications at all and testified to almost everyone I met of how God had kept me in the palm of his hand and was healing my body. Three weeks later I was taken off the Glyburide, since my blood sugars continued to drop too low. My doctor said she had never seen anyone's blood sugar drop at such a dramatic rate and for them to come off all medications in such a short period of time. She agreed with me that God continues to heal me.

'I continued to praise the Lord and keep myself covered in prayer. Two months after being in such a critical state that I should have died, I was no longer on any medication.'

Today Brendalyn continues to prosper and gives all the glory to God for maintaining her. With his guidance she keeps her blood sugars under control with diet and exercise only. She concludes, 'I know that my prayers and those of my family and friends are the reason I am alive and well today.'

'The Lord is near to all who call on him,
to all who call on him in truth.
He fulfils the desires of those who fear him;
he hears their cry and saves them.'

Psalm 145:18-19

Chapter 4

Hope again

'For I know the plans I have for you,' declares the Lord, 'plans to prosper you and not to harm you, plans to give you hope and a future.'
Jeremiah 29:11, 12

'If I can only touch the hem of his garment, I will be made whole.' What tremendous words of faith! The Scriptures declare in Mark 5:25 that this woman had been suffering for twelve years. She had tried everything available to her in order to receive healing, yet to no avail. It would seem that having tried for so long her natural, human response would have been discouragement and despair which would have banished any further hope. Yet despite twelve years of disappointment, when Jesus finally came her way, even in the midst of her despair, she rose to the challenge to hope again.

The Scriptures tell us in Jeremiah 29:11 that God has plans, 'plans to give you hope and a future'. Gary Zarback discovered the miraculous effect of rekindling such a renewed hope in God.

In 1998 Gary was diagnosed with terminal nasopharnyx cancer, an invasive brain tumour of terrible malignancy. He described himself, a former Buddhist dropout, devoid of faith in God, as one without hope and, at 117 pounds, deteriorating in health. He confessed that the only things he still possessed was a terrifying fear of dying, and the strong, steady love of his wife and sons.

'In my fifty-nine years of life, I'd been many things – a father of six children, a musician, a long-time drug addict and hustler (living my life in the fast lane), and a confirmed agnostic. So, there I was at the end of my life – too soon! I was full of love, but still spiritually barren and crying my heart out. But you know what happened? Yes, the Lord made himself known to me and Jesus Christ came into my life, at last! I, Gary Z., was born again!

'I was totally bed-bound, barely alive, my mortal nutrition flowing through tubes in my body. I had lost the swallow reflex several months before, so I had been unable to consume normal food, but spiritual nutrition was flowing into my body from all directions! People I'd never met or seen were praying for me in a little church across the state, thanks to one of my loving sisters-in-law!

'Although I couldn't leave my bed, being hooked to a morphine pump twenty-four hours a day to relieve the constant agony of the hungry tumour in my head, my heart began filling with hope. Hope! An idea that had become foreign to me. I was going deaf, losing my vision and preparing to die, but now that God was in my life I was no longer terrified of dying. With my hand in the Lord's, I was ready to die with dignity and at peace.

'New strength continued to pour into me. With help I became able to leave my bed and walk a bit every day, and I began regaining my lost weight: 117, 120, 122 pounds. I began attending the small neighbourhood church for the very first time in my life. I regained 125, 128lbs, and my swallow reflex began working again, and I was able to taste my first honest-to-goodness food for the first time in over seven months. I reached 135, 140, 145lbs and I eventually began riding a mountain bike, a few blocks a day at first, increasing to twenty miles every day. Still the weight kept pouring onto my once ravaged and wasted body.

'By the time July 1998 rolled around, which was the month I should have died, my weight was at 160lbs and I was able to play my beloved music again. This time it was in church with my 18-year-old son David.

'And still my weight increased: 165, 175, 190lbs. My doctor, a top specialist in the field of oncology, was amazed, not having seen me since his diagnosis nine months previously. Eighty wonderful pounds of healthy, living flesh had miraculously rejoined my once doomed and dying body. I prayed and praised and gave still more prayer and thanks! I got baptised in a loving church, attended several revivals, and brought some old "friends" from the other side of the tracks to God and to church.

'And before I knew it, I was celebrating my 60th birthday. Praise the Lord! The feeding tube has been removed, and at present I'm eating normally again. I'm nearly totally off the morphine and other drugs I was so dependent on to save my life from misery and pain, and it is now almost a virtual certainty; the brain tumour inside my head is now dead. It is no longer destroying the wonderful body God had provided for me. It is no longer the root of all my fears and uncertainties. It is now just a hidden, ugly, scarred mass of inert tissue residing in my head, unnoticed, but never to be forgotten by me or my friends and family.

'I have much more than my life back: I also have the Lord in my life, and the knowledge of the price Jesus paid for me and for you to be free. I truly have a hope again. Praise God!'

Gary's story is a wonderful testimony to the way hope in the Almighty God has the power to provide a resurgence of healing. The Psalmist David said, 'Happy is he who has the God of Jacob for his help, whose hope is in the Lord' (Ps. 146:5, NKJV). Gary's experience reveals the assurance that God is just as willing to restore the sick now as when the Holy Spirit spoke those words through the psalmist. In God there is a healing balm for every disease, restoring power for every infirmity. His desire for every human being is expressed in the words,

'Beloved, I pray that you may prosper in all things and be in health, just as your soul prospers.'
3 John 2, NKJV

Andrea Tawney also shared that desire. She was diagnosed with an illness called Systemic Erythematosus Lupus, a long-term debilitation involving joints, skin, and potentially all major organs. Andrea tells her dramatic healing story.

'It was the early fall of 1981. I was just a month into my first classroom teaching job in our brand-new Christian school. I had the split third/fourth grade and a teaching partner. I usually taught Sunday school, Vacation Bible school, youth groups, at camps and in women's classes. Christian day school was an exciting new venture.

'The lupus symptoms started simply enough. I was supervising students during lunch break and an out-of-control basketball came my way. It knocked into the back of my right hand, jarring it. It stung, but was too minor to pay attention to. The next day my hand was stiff. A week later the joints in my fingers were still painful, and within just a couple of weeks my elbow, hip, and knee on the right side were sore. No amount of aspirin stopped the discomfort so it was time to have the doctor check it out.

'He tested for rheumatoid arthritis but that showed

negative. So he sent me to a specialist. This doctor did extensive tests and finally diagnosed lupus. It was a tentative diagnosis, since this seemed to be a rather vague sort of disease. The typical analgesic-type arthritis medications were prescribed, but, aside from causing stomach upset, had little effect. The joint pain increased, and the medications were adjusted. As the medications got stronger, the stomach pain got stronger and the joint pain grew worse.

'As soon as the diagnosis of lupus was made, my husband and I asked for prayer from our church, friends not affiliated to our church, and family in the United States and Canada. Both my husband and I had been Christians since our teens, and we were fully confident that it was within God's ability to heal me. Whether or not, in his sovereignty, he would, we didn't know, but we would trust him to do the best for our family.

'As the weeks went by, the pain increased. Many people prayed for me, laid hands on me, anointed me with oil, and encouraged me constantly. The pain became so severe I could no longer clap during worship. It hurt to hold a pen or lift a book – which for a teacher is a disaster. We bought a compact style of Bible because I could not carry or even hold my study version. I used both hands to pick up bottles, cups or items of any weight. It hurt to walk, sit or stand. Even the weight of the sheet on my feet at night was painful.

'While to my friends and family the Lord seemed to be speaking of healing and encouragement, to me he said, "Yea, though I walk through the valley of the shadow of death, I will fear no evil; for you are with me; your rod and your staff, they comfort me." (Ps. 23:4, NKJV.) I didn't find that so very encouraging, but I knew I could trust him. My husband and I were both sure that with such rapid development of the disease, if God didn't heal me, I would soon be in serious trouble. In the world's understanding, my prognosis was not good.

'During the following autumn, I attended a seminar on healing with a number of friends. They were filled with the highest hopes for my healing. I was not experiencing hopefulness; I was probably more resigned. Pain and coping seemed to fill my time and take up all my energy. I knew God would do what he would do and that was enough for me. At the seminar God dealt with me powerfully in the area of forgiveness. We saw miracles of physical healing that day, but none was for me. My healing was emotional and spiritual and, while it was a wonderfully exciting day, I was still in pain.

'The holidays came and went, the pain came and stayed, and I grew more and more fatigued. In the New Year our church planned a seminar on worship. A powerful worship leader came to teach. The Friday night seminar was excellent, and during the ministry time I received prayer. While God spoke to my heart, there was nothing from him for my body.

'On the Saturday night, during the ministry time again, I received prayer. This time the Holy Spirit overwhelmed me physically. I could barely stand; my body felt heavily limp. I couldn't move and was hardly able to breathe. I could feel my body being drained of something, with powerful waves flowing down from my head to my feet. I knew without a doubt that the lupus was leaving me, and a tremendous relief filled me. I didn't say much; I couldn't say much!

'The next day at church I could clap during worship with the best of the clappers and everyone rejoiced with me. I returned to the doctor, and as he checked each of my joints there was no pain. I was able to grip his hand strongly, when prior to this I could not grip at all. I told him that God had healed me through the prayers of my Christian friends, and all he could say was, "Well, tell your friends they did you good!" I never returned to the doctor.

'I remembered the words God had spoken to me about the valley of the shadow of death, and I realised that I had focused on being in the valley. I hadn't seen that the valley was filled with shadows, nothing real, and that the promise was that I would pass through. My faith in God's *ability and desire to heal me* never wavered. My faith that he *would heal me* wobbled constantly. I could only cling to his love, and the sure knowledge that, in his sovereignty, he would do what was best for my family and me.'

Because of the steadfast prayers from everyone around Andrea, her eyes were fixed on the Lord and on his faithfulness. What matters is not what he does for and with us, but that he *is*. Just knowing this is enough. He hears us and chooses in his almighty wisdom, generously mixed with love and grace, what is best for us. Our challenge is to hope on, even when our surroundings seem dark or dismal. The Scriptures assure us,

> ***'"Call to me and I will answer you and tell you great and unsearchable things you do not know."'***
>
> *Jeremiah 33:3*

Veronica Neybert found her spirituality challenged one day when she received an unexpected call from her doctor. There was a sense of urgency in his voice as he reported that the results of her mammograms needed to be discussed. The doctor wanted to schedule an appointment with the radiologist for a biopsy to determine if the spots on the mammograms were cancerous. The impact of the call, implying as it did the possibility of cancer, began to hit home.

The challenge to Veronica's faith became more daunting as she realised that cancer was something that had run through her family. Her sister had died at the age of 40 from cancer. Her father, grandmother and other members of her family had various kinds of cancer. It was rampant in the family on both her father's and mother's sides. Her mother had had a lumpectomy for a cancerous breast tumour. Amid all these revolving thoughts, she knew that this was not a time to panic and think of what might happen. It was a time to pray.

'I shared my problem with a few trusted friends. It was decided to have an evening of special prayer, with the laying on of hands, asking for God's mercy and healing touch. We spent time in praise and worship. After confessing our sins and receiving his forgiveness we laid our petitions before Jesus. I was anointed with blessed oil and stood on God's word in Exodus 23:25: *"Worship the Lord your God, and his blessing will be on your food and water. I will take away sickness from among you."*

'I reminded the Lord that by his stripes we are healed and that *"with him all things are possible"*. During the prayer time a deep sense of peace and warmth covered my body. I knew in my heart that everything would be all right. I still had to walk in faith and see how Jesus was going to deal with the cancer.

'I visited the surgeon's office and had my pre-operation physical and all the necessary blood work done for the surgical procedure. The following week I went back to him for my final check-up before surgery. Before leaving his office I asked him if I could pray with him. He said, "Yes, I'm a Christian." I told him I would not consent to surgery unless I first prayed over him and asked God to guide him and give him the necessary wisdom to make the correct choices for my medical condition. After a moment of prayer, he thanked me and said that he really appreciated my praying with him. It was the first time he had ever had a patient pray with him.

'Two days later I was in the wheelchair waiting for surgery. "When are you going to act, God? Or are they going to find the tumours are benign? I really don't want to go through the biopsies and the pain, etc. Let your will be done, Lord."

'A nurse came to get me. She wheeled me into the x-ray room instead of surgery because they needed to do another mammogram. I saw my old mammograms with the little spots circled on them on the wall in front of me. I dragged myself with all my tubes and went through the procedures again. The technician asked me to sit on the chair and wait until they examined this set of mammograms. I told her not to worry; I couldn't go too far dragging my tubes, barefoot and dressed in a gown split open down the back!

'I was beginning to feel giddy by then. I prayed and asked our Lord how and when he would honour his word. "I just don't want to go through surgery," I kept saying to the Lord. After a long wait, the technician returned with the radiologist. "I am recommending that surgery be cancelled." I threw up my arms and yelled, "Thank you, Jesus. Praise your holy name! Thank you!" The radiologist looked at me as if I'd lost my mind. The technician appeared to be angry, but the cute little black LPN gave me the high sign and had a grin from ear to ear. As I went down the hall back to the holding area, I yelled, "Jesus healed me!" The surgeon came in and said that he would have to check the new mammogram and talk to the radiologist. After looking at the mammograms, he agreed that there was no need for surgery.

'I went home, and after sharing the news with my brother-in-law, who is a doctor, I found out that they just don't do last-minute repeat mammograms before surgery. But they had! It was divine intervention. God's ways certainly are not my ways but, thank God, he is looking after me and guiding me as I walk the path he has laid out for me. I can do all things when Jesus Christ is my strength.'

Since then, Veronica has had no recurrence of cysts or tumours in her breasts. Her annual mammograms have all been normal and she continues to experience a fulfilled hope in the God of all Hope.

'We wait in hope for the Lord; he is our help and our shield. In him our hearts rejoice, for we trust in his holy name. May your unfailing love rest upon us, O Lord, even as we put our hope in you.'

Psalm 33:20-22

Chapter 5

A renewed journey

'I will lead the blind by ways they have not known,
along unfamiliar paths I will guide them;
I will turn the darkness into light before them
and make the rough places smooth.
These are the things I will do; I will not forsake them.'
Isaiah 42:16

It must have been humbling being told that to be healed you must wash seven times in a murky river. Yet this was the experience of Naaman, the Syrian captain (2 Kings 5:1-14). The Scriptures describe him as a 'great man,' a 'valiant soldier' and 'highly regarded'. But he had leprosy. In order to be healed this mighty soldier would have to subject himself to the miry waters of the River Jordan.

These words of healing instruction given by Elisha, were relayed to Naaman by a messenger. 'Surely,' Naaman thought, 'this man of God could at least see me himself! . . . and stand and call on the name of the Lord his God, wave his hand over the spot and cure me of my leprosy' (2 Kings 5:11).

When we think of healing we often imagine an instantaneous occurrence. Although there are experiences when this happens, oftentimes a period of healing may involve travelling on an unmapped journey when only God knows the ultimate destination. A journey on which lessons such as trust, humility, faith and forgiveness are learnt. You could imagine that after washing three times and seeing no improvement, Naaman was ready to give up. After all, this was humiliation! The sixth wash, still no change – the shame and embarrassment. It's in times like these that the challenge is to 'Let go and let God.' The Psalmist captures this challenge when he says, *' "Be still, and know that I am God" '* Ps. 46:10.

God was leading Naaman upon a journey of healing on which he was to learn to be still in the presence of God and experience humility and trust in God.

The seventh wash, and the Scriptures declare, 'his flesh was restored and became clean like that of a young boy' (2 Kings 5:14). Much patience is called for in the journey of healing.

Carolyn Scheidies is one who embarked upon such a patient journey. It was thirty years before she returned to her school where she recalled the tragic events that led to her debilitating disease. Now she had returned as the guest speaker.

'I marvelled that I was there at all. I'd returned walking. Of all people, I'd been asked to speak at this special combined service celebrating my 30th High School reunion. It was a holiday weekend in 1999, and I'd returned a success. They had all rejoiced with me, the author of 11 books with hundreds of other published credits. They rejoiced because 30 years earlier I had been confined to a wheelchair.

'It began one January, after a serious bout of strep throat and just before my 13th birthday. I began to feel as though I'd been run over by a truck. I hurt all over. My arms and legs didn't want to move.

'To say I was scared would be too mild. By the time school ended that spring, everyone knew something was wrong. I was active. I was a tomboy. I loved to run and play. I loved being outdoors. Suddenly I found excuses to stay indoors, found reasons not to participate in activities which caused me pain. I tried to hide all the pain and terror – but I failed. Even the other students, my friends, realised something was wrong.

'Concerned, my parents took me to the doctor. After a battery of tests the results came back – Juvenile Rheumatoid Arthritis. So began a long journey for me. Within a year I was in a wheelchair, despite every effort to keep my legs straight. My parents took me from doctor to doctor, from one rehabilitation centre to another where I got varying degrees of help. I always battled pain and depression and the belief that I wasn't of use to anyone. Furthermore, I felt I was a burden to everyone.

'During that time, there were many caring people who prayed for me. However, there were many unanswered questions in my mind. Why didn't God answer in the way I wanted? Why wasn't he listening? I'd ask my father. He just told me to trust God. But I knew my parents were hurting as much as I was.

'At night when all was still, when an owl hooted outside my window, when a lone coyote howled in the distance, when sleep evaded me, more and more I'd play with ideas and words and couplets until a poem or song took shape in my mind. Over and over I'd try to impress it on my mind. With my legs and hands encased in splints, I was helpless to write my creations on paper. What I did have were very understanding parents. "Mum. Dad," I'd call in the dead of night. One or the other would stumble into the room, sit down and pick up paper and pen and write down my poem, or song. The next morning there it was, a creation born out of my own deep hurts, my searching, my pain.

'Little did I realise that my illness released me to write reams of poems and songs and other things which spoke to my situation. It honed my writing skills and ignited my desire to write as a career. I also began to learn that God was more than the sum of my wants. Though I didn't realise it, God wasn't finished with me yet. A few years later, my father drove me hundreds of miles to a conference where he knew they prayed for the sick. On the way we broke the trip into two days because I couldn't handle travelling for long periods of time.

'The services were uplifting. I felt encouraged, but sceptical. After all, I was used to all sorts of individuals and ministers praying for me. Sometimes I felt I was their latest challenge. However, this time something was different. The last day when Dad took me up to the front the minister looked at me and said, "I've been fasting and praying for you this week." As I stared at him, he placed his hand gently on my head and began to pray.

'Suddenly I felt as though a hundred locks opened. The pain disappeared. God healed me of the active disease. My legs didn't straighten. My hands didn't look any less gnarled, but at that moment I began to improve.

'Back at the motel Dad tried to get me to take my painkillers, but I refused. "I don't need them," I told him. And I didn't. For the first time in a long time, I spent a peaceful, rest-filled night. The next morning we started home. What a difference! Instead of lying in the back seat gritting my teeth, I sat up and enjoyed the passing scenery. Instead of waiting for the trip to end, I said, "Let's keep going. I'm doing fine." And I was. We drove all the way home without staying over.

'In the next months and years, I learned to dress myself and pretty much take care of my personal needs. But I was still tied to the wheelchair, a wheelchair I was not strong enough to wheel myself. Different rehabilitation centres suggested a variety of treatments, which did little to straighten my legs. Surgery was hesitantly suggested, but there were no guarantees that any of the surgical techniques available at the time would have lasting benefits. They did suggest straightening my legs, but then they would not have been able to bend. That would bring on a whole new set of problems. The answer was "No."

'When we moved to Iowa, Margaret Freeman, an author from our church, took me under her wing. She helped me sell my first story, and my writing career began. By this time I'd set my sights on a journalism degree.

'The college I attended wasn't as accessible as today's standards demand, but it was good enough for me at the time. It was while I was there that I met Dr Ellis who wanted to help me. Joint replacements had hit the medical establishment. The problem was that they were guaranteed for only seven to ten years. That's why their use at the time was confined to the elderly. I was in my early twenties. Joint replacement surgery might get me up and walking. It would also almost certainly guarantee that I'd need surgery in the future.

'Dr Ellis went out of his way to secure funding for the massive reconstructive surgery involved in helping me get back on my feet. He even took my x-rays to the founder of the then new procedure of total joint replacement to make sure he'd do the very best for me.

'I was hesitant, scared. What if I couldn't do all the things I could already do? What if this procedure made things worse for me? What if? Patiently Dr Ellis answered my questions. He loved the Lord and he cared what happened to me. He advised surgery. My own prayers led me to the same conclusion. Finally, the summer after I graduated from college, I checked into the hospital. I had visions of gracefully walking out of the hospital, smiling at all those who had looked down on the "poor girl in the wheelchair".

'More than anything, what Dr Ellis gave me was hope, but what I had not envisaged were weeks of surgery and the various rehabilitation techniques required to get the new joints to work. Not even Dr Ellis realised until he got started what it would take to get me back on my feet. I had not envisaged weeks and months of healing and pain and relearning how to walk with full-length leg braces and crutches. I had not envisaged all the determination I would need to stay the course. Nor had I envisaged the wonderful friends who would help me along the way, who would pray with and for me, who would encourage and support me, including one special person.

'One year after my surgery, I walked down the aisle of our little church without crutches, without braces, to take the hand of the man who became my husband, a man who accepted me just the way I was. And though the years brought more surgery – another set of knees, four hip replacements, two ankle fusions – they also brought two beautiful children by Caesarean section.

'The young girl who had looked upon herself as a burden, now 30 years later stood in front of the congregation at my school as the guest speaker. What she saw – what *I* saw – was a good God who works through my failures and my pain to give me a platform to reach out to other hurting people.

'What I *know* is that God is in control, and I'm glad I belong to him.'

'But they that wait upon the Lord shall renew their strength; they shall mount up with wings as eagles; they shall run, and not be weary; and they shall walk, and not faint.'

Isaiah 40:31, KJV

Eva Eveson also embarked on a journey of a different kind. At four months pregnant she wondered if she would ever be able to behold her miracle child.

' "Ahhhh!" I screamed as I raised my hands to cover my face and slammed on the brakes. A blinding hot flame shot through my eyes. "God, help me," I prayed silently. Tears began to course down my cheeks and I was able to open my eyes just enough to focus on the road ahead.

'The drive home was a nightmare. I immediately removed my contact lenses. I hadn't worn glasses in years; I didn't even own a spare pair, but I figured if I rested my eyes a bit I'd be okay. I was wrong.

'For the next several weeks I kept silent as the recurring pain came upon me each time I went out into the sunshine. I wore sunglasses all day, even inside my home. I don't know why I was afraid to tell someone that I was having a problem. Perhaps I thought the sensitivity to light was a part of my pregnancy.

'One day my eyes began to pour thick mucus. Then I noticed that having to wear my sunglasses went way into the evening. At night the light from the television was too much for me. One afternoon, I pulled a blanket over my head and cried. It was time to admit that this was not normal and to say something to my husband.

'The following day he drove me to an ophthalmologist's office where I was given a diagnosis I have yet to remember. It was three very long words – that I do remember! The doctor tried to sound optimistic, but his words left me shaking.

' "I'm going to dilate your eyes," he began. "Then I'll put a patch on your right eye. That's the one I'm most concerned about. I want you to put these drops in both eyes three times a day, and keep this eye patch on unless you're sleeping."

' "Am I going to lose my vision?" I asked.

' "I'm not as concerned about your left eye as I am your right," he said, avoiding the question. "I only wish you had come in sooner."

'At this point I should have been well acquainted with God and his healing power and miraculous handiwork. The very fact that I was four months pregnant was a miracle. The previous September, after months of gynaecological difficulties, I had undergone exploratory surgery to determine exactly what my problem was. I had conceived three times before, but never made it to the second trimester. My doctors told me that I had endometriosis. They said, "Your uterus is in such a state as to make it nearly impossible to get pregnant, much less carry to term.'

'I had two stepchildren whom I loved dearly, but I wanted one of my own! My mother, who stood behind me, gently placed her hand on my shoulder and said, "Where's your faith?" I nodded. "God," I prayed. "if you want me to get pregnant, then make me pregnant. If you don't, give me the understanding of your will." Six days later, I conceived.

'This small wonder was growing inside me, but my new fear was that I would not be able to see the baby I had so longed for. After the doctor had examined my eyes I spent the next three weeks literally in blind confusion. I couldn't see well enough to read. I couldn't study my Bible. The days seemed to drag on forever.

'Somewhere in this three-week interim, my mother came for a visit. She repeated the same words she had spoken a few months before. "Where is your faith?" I honestly couldn't answer that. With God's recent move in my life, one would think that I would have just said, "Oh, but of course! OK, God. Heal me!" But the pain was so real and the situation seemed somehow bigger than he was. This time I would have to rely on the faith of my mother. She and I prayed together. And, within three weeks, my eyes were back to "normal". I had not lost any vision in either eye! However, the doctor insis-ted that I stay away from contact lens for a while and wear glasses exclusively. I wasn't happy, my vanity being what it was, but I agreed.

'In June 1981, a beautiful baby girl with soft blonde hair and large blue eyes was born just forty minutes into her due date. It was nine months to the day since I had been told that pregnancy and delivery would be impossible. For nine months I had secretly prayed for a little girl with blonde hair and blue eyes. God had given me the desire of my heart and the eyes with which to see her.

'That year the problem with my eyes recurred. The diagnosis was the same. The prognosis was as dim as it had been the first time. But this time, my attitude about faith and healing was different.

' "I want to see you in a week," the doctor told me.

'Ironically, my mother was due for a visit that day. As soon as she walked into the room I told her about my doctor's visit. "There's a prayer session tonight at the church," I told her. "I can go and have the elders, deacons, and prayer warriors anoint me and pray for me. Do you want to come with me?"

' "Absolutely!" Mother exclaimed positively.

'The following week I marched into the doctor's office, jumped into the chair and exclaimed, "You won't find anything wrong with these eyes, Dr Sanders. These eyes are perfectly healed."

' "I don't think so," he said from across the room. He switched the light off and walked toward me. "I'm not expecting a complete healing for several weeks. But hopefully most of the blisters are gone."

' "You don't understand," I told him. "There will be no blisters because I gave this over to God and he has healed me once and for all!"

'Dr Sanders pointed the light of his ophthalmoscope toward me. "Uh-huh. We'll see about – Huh! My goodness!"

'I grinned. "They're gone, aren't they?"

' "They sure are," he said sounding rather surprised.

' "Told you," I said, still grinning.

' "I don't know that I believe in the God thing," he replied, as he sat back down at his desk.

' "Well, I do," I responded, full of confidence, 'and right now, that's all that really matters, isn't it?" '

Eva's journey led her to a renewed strength in God. Today she is the author of a number of books and through her established ministry of intercessory prayer has become a channel of strength in encouraging others on their spiritual journey.

'But for you who revere my name, the sun of righteousness will rise with healing in its wings.'
Malachi 4:2

Betty Huff's most dramatic healing by prayer occurred in 1954 after the birth of her second daughter, Kathleen. Her pregnancy at age 21 was normal until her waters broke six weeks early. Unlike a normal labour, the placenta began to break apart (placenta abruptio) and an emergency Caesarean section was performed. That was the beginning of her nightmare ordeal. Betty recalls that only fervent prayers from many different denominations saved her and the baby. (Kathleen is now the grandmother of four.)

'After the delivery, the doctor told my husband that he had lost the baby and gave me only a fifty-fifty chance to live. Later, the baby began to breathe on her own, but my life hung in the balance for the next three months. Six weeks after the birth I had a massive post-partum haemorrhage with blood pouring from every bodily orifice. Six orderlies had to run to the operating room, each holding an I.V. of whole blood flowing into my unconscious body.

'A hysterectomy was performed vaginally and the problem seemed to be solved. Two weeks later another massive haemorrhage tore out all the stitches and I was given only oxygen during the mop-up and repair for fear that in my weakened state anaesthetic might kill me. At that point my Christian doctor began some serious research coupled with prayer. Also praying were my Catholic family, my Jewish in-laws, our Baptist landlords and our Seventh-day Adventist neighbours.

'Another two weeks, another haemorrhage. My doctor flew from California to Chicago and found good news and bad news. The bad news was that there had been only three cases like mine in the prior ten-year period and all three women had died. The good news was that they knew it was caused by a lack of fibrogen (blood clotting agent) in the blood. The lack of fibrogen was caused by my not eating enough protein. (My only source of dietary protein had been an occasional peanut butter sandwich and a glass of milk.)

'My doctor flew home with a tiny vial of protein-enriched plasma. My final haemorrhage occurred that evening and the life-giving vial was attached to the cannula in my arm. I came out of my comatose state the next morning. The room was flooded with sunshine, the birds were chirping and my mother was singing "Happy birthday to you". I was 22 that day!'

Sometimes the journey of healing in itself can be a painful one. It may involve much despair and emotional scarring on the way. During such times we look at the example of Christ, who ultimately took upon himself *our* personal journey of life and lived a life which was ours so that we can live a life which is his. Isaiah reminds us of the path he trod before us.

'He was despised and rejected by men, a man of sorrows, and familiar with suffering. Like one from whom men hide their faces he was despised, and we esteemed him not.

'Surely he took up our infirmities and carried our sorrows, yet we considered him stricken by God, smitten by him, and afflicted.

'But he was pierced for our transgressions, he was crushed for our iniquities; the punishment that brought us peace was upon him, and by his wounds we are healed.

'We all, like sheep, have gone astray, each of us has turned to his own way; and the Lord has laid on him the iniquity of us all.

'He was oppressed and afflicted, yet he did not open his mouth; he was led like a lamb to the slaughter, and as a sheep before her shearers is silent, so he did not open his mouth.

'By oppression and judgment he was taken away.
And who can speak of his descendants?
For he was cut off from the land of the living;
for the transgression of my people he was stricken.'

Isaiah 53:3-8

Chapter 6

I do a new thing

'See, I am doing a new thing! Now it springs up; do you not perceive it? I am making a way in the desert and streams in the wasteland.'

Isaiah 43:19

Imagine what it must have been like for Hannah. There was a woman who desperately wanted a child of her own. With each passing year the possibilities seemed more and more remote. Others constantly provoked her because of her barrenness, and despite the love of her husband, the Scriptures portray her as a woman who experienced much grief and 'bitterness of soul', who 'wept much,' and was of a 'sorrowful spirit' (1 Sam. 1:10, 15).

At a time when Hannah could have allowed such discouragement to cause her to abandon her faith, the Scriptures reveal how in the midst of her mental anguish she turned to God in prayer.

' "O Lord Almighty, if you will only look upon your servant's misery and remember me, and not forget your servant but give her a son, then I will give him to the Lord for all the days of his life, and no razor will ever be used on his head" ' (1 Sam. 1:11).

Her prayer was answered: ' "I prayed for this child, and the Lord has granted me what I asked of him" ' (1 Sam. 1:27).

The Lord was able to 'do a new thing' for Hannah, and make what was initially a barren experience become, *'a way in the desert and streams in the wasteland'*.

One of the blessed assurances for a Christian is to know that whatever circumstance may occur in life, with God *'all things are possible'*. It is a comforting assurance to know, yet at the same time also to understand that *'God's ways are not our ways neither his thoughts our thoughts'* (see Isaiah 55:8). Hence God in his infinite wisdom knows in every given situation what is best for us. That whatever besetment may come our way, God is in control.

This was a lesson which David and Sherene Harper were to learn. I first met them while pastoring a church in Trowbridge in England. They were both keen and active members. They had been married for four years and in that time had been trying for a baby. During my pastorate with them, I saw their dejection and disheartenment when it seemed all attempts for a child failed. They share their story.

'The wonders of God became a reality in my life when I met David in Jamaica, the home of my birth, in 1990. While he was on holiday we fell in love and got married in 1993. We set up our home in England.

'We started to try for a family a year after we got married. With no success we went to see our doctor. From there we were sent to see a specialist. We had some tests done, and the results showed that I had a blocked tube. We would never be able to have children naturally. I was told I would need an operation to clear the tube.

'After the operation in 1997 we were told that the tube was badly damaged. Added to this there was only a 10 per cent chance for me to conceive, but if it didn't happen in the first year after the operation my chances would be nil. Our only choice would be IVF. My chances of conceiving naturally would be one in a million.

'It was very hard for me to accept. I cried every day. I felt ashamed of myself, together with the thought of letting David down. I wouldn't talk about the problem. I didn't let my family know. I was so depressed I even tried to take my life on two occasions. I tried to push David away from me. I told him to go and find someone who could give him children. His parents told him to leave me, because a married couple ought to have children. His answer to me all the time was that he married me because he loved me, not because I could give him children.

'Despite all this, David and I grew closer to each other. He was there more for me than I was for him. I sometimes told him it was my problem but he always said it was *our* problem. I forgot sometimes that he was just as hurt as I was.

'We had our first attempt at IVF in 1998. It didn't work and we tried again in 1999. Again it was a failure. We had spent more than £7,500 on IVF treatment, not including time off work without pay.

'During that time I didn't know who I was or what I believed in. I lost touch with the Lord. After prayer I would get up off my knees feeling the same way I went down – with an oppressed heart.

'It was when we decided to adopt that I started to accept that I would never be able to give birth to a child. One day I was talking about adoption at work, saying that my heart was not 100 per cent in it, because I wanted to give birth to a child of my own. One of my work mates said, "It's not an egg and sperm from a partner that makes you good parents; it's the love you show and give to children." I thought about what she said and my heart was more inclined towards adoption.

'I read 1 Samuel 1:1-28 and 1 Samuel 2:1-2. I felt how Hannah was feeling when she was praying to the Lord.

That night I got up from my knees in prayer feeling a different person. It was as if a burden had been lifted from me. From that night I didn't feel bitter any more when I saw children in the streets or when people talked about their children. If David told me that he loved me I believed him.

'When we were accepted for the adoption process, we booked a holiday for three weeks in Jamaica. We were going to tell our family about the problems we were having, together with the decision to adopt a child.

'Two weeks before our holiday, David kept telling me that I was pregnant. I had stopped taking notice of when my periods were due and I took no notice of what he was saying. He kept asking me to take a home pregnancy test. Finally I took the test and in my anger threw it at him. I didn't even look at the results. I heard David crying, saying, "Yes! Thank you, God." I didn't believe the results. I took four more tests. All were positive. That night I didn't sleep. I prayed, giving thanks to the Lord.

'I had a wonderful nine months of pregnancy. I went into labour one week early. During that time, the baby's heartbeat dropped from 171 to 50. The doctor was worried about the heartbeat and he called in four more doctors to check. We told them that everything would be fine because the baby was a miracle baby; the Lord had given us the baby and nothing was going to be wrong.

'I gave birth to a healthy baby girl, and we called her Shania Alisha Sherene Harper. It had taken us six years to have a child, but the Lord had answered our prayers. We now have a closer relationship with him. David and I are closer to each other, too, and Shania gives us more love and joy each day than we can ever give to her.

'We thank the Lord each day for answering our prayers and fulfilling our dream. We have enough proof that what is impossible for man is possible for the Lord.'

'Weeping may remain for a night,
but rejoicing comes in the morning.'
Psalm 30:5

Another person who can testify to God's unfailing power is Ken Haynes. About fifteen years ago he was injured while trying to arrest a drug suspect. At the time, he was a police officer in southern California. The injury he sustained was to his right arm, shoulder, neck and back of his head. Since then, he suffered from migraine headaches that became more and more severe as the years went by.

'It was a severe enough injury to force me to leave the police department, and I moved to Portland, Oregon, seeking work in the computer industry.

'About two years ago the pain became constant. Each day I was in terrible agony and at least two to three times a week I was rushed to Accident and Emergency with pain so bad I was throwing up. During these episodes I was extremely sound sensitive, and even the sound of someone breathing in the same room was excruciating.

'After I had been through what seemed like the entire medicine chest, the doctors put me on 130mg of oral morphine just to keep the baseline pain levels low enough for me to function.

' "During this whole time my wife Kelly had been praying constantly for my healing and relief, but it seemed that, like the apostle Paul, I was to have a "thorn in my side", and that I would have to bear it the rest of my life. We never gave up hope of finding a cure, or that the Lord would heal me. We continued to press on with prayer and ask the Lord for guidance and healing.

'One day I read an article in one of the medical journals I subscribe to, about a condition known as cervicogenic headache (CH), caused by injury to the neck. This is a common headache among whiplash victims of car accidents.

'I searched high and low for a doctor in my health maintenance organisation who knew anything about CH. No one seemed to know anything. I printed article after article from the Internet, and took them to my doctors and specialists in a vain attempt to get them to diagnose and treat my condition. They all dismissed the reports and told me that they knew best what to do.

'Over the Internet we found a clinic in Toronto, Canada, that seemed to know something about CH. I called them, and they said that I would have to travel to the clinic in order to get a diagnosis. We prayed, "Lord, if it is your will for us to go to Canada, please make it possible."

'We put out the word to our friends that we were thinking about going to Canada to get the diagnosis made, and we asked them to pray that the Lord would open doors of opportunity for us to be able to go.

'A friend called us a couple of days after we'd put out the prayer request, and told us that his boss had accumulated enough frequent flyer miles to provide us with two first-class return tickets to Toronto at no cost to us! We were flabbergasted! He also said that since he travelled to Toronto on a regular basis, he had an apartment there. He would normally have been there during that period of the year, but it just so happened that he would be on vacation elsewhere, so we could have his apartment – and stay there rent free! WOW! What a miracle and a wonderful blessing! That was miracle number one.

'The Canadian doctors told us that we would have to be there for a couple of days, and that it would probably cost us around $2,000 for the initial interview at their clinic for a diagnosis.

'Meanwhile, without telling us, some other friends had

been collecting money to purchase our airline tickets. We'd expected to have to take out a loan for those and the visit to the clinic, and we were willing to do that, but the Lord had other plans.

'Then several other friends sent us money, too. The total amount collected completely covered our expenses, including food, the rental car, and even the $2,000 payable to the clinic! That was miracle number two.

'We went to Toronto, and the diagnosis was confirmed. I had the condition. The doctors in Canada told us that there was a good doctor in the US (in Minneapolis) who would be able to take my case. We decided that the Lord had obviously put us on this path and we would see where it would lead us. We were going to Minneapolis. We didn't know how we were going to get there, but we were sure that if the Lord wanted us to be in Minneapolis, he'd surely find a way.

'When we were on our way home, we discovered that we could catch an earlier flight if we hurried. Excited at the thought of getting home earlier, we jumped at the chance and were on our way home.

'While on this flight,(one that we really shouldn't have been on), I struck up a conversation with a gentlemen in the seat across the aisle from me. I found that he was going home after being in the Caribbean for a week or so. He was a personable gentleman, and he asked me where I'd been. I simply told him I'd been to Toronto for medical reasons. He seemed curious about what medical condition could have caused me to go all the way to Toronto to get a diagnosis, so I told him about CH and that the only people I could find to do the diagnosis and treatment were the folks in Toronto. He asked me if I was going to have a particular type of surgery done to correct the problem, which took me completely by surprise because it was the correct type of surgery. I asked him what he did for a living, and he told me that he was a doctor at the pain management centre at the Oregon Health Sciences University in Portland, Oregon, and that not only was he very familiar with my condition, he could probably treat it as well! That was miracle number three.

'Needless to say, I was very excited and I got his name and number and immediately took the diagnosis from Canada and the doctor's name back to my Health Maintenance Organisation to ask for a referral. The doctor on the airplane even supplied me with further published articles (which my doctors read later), that supported the diagnosis from Canada.

'After some red tape (that the Lord cut through quickly), I was in the office of the doctor I'd met on the plane, and he was doing further (more specific) tests to determine exactly what type of treatment I would need.

'Soon, it was confirmed by Oregon Health Sciences University that I had CH, and they decided that I would need a C2 Dorsal Nerve Root Ganglionectomy. I was referred to neuro-surgery for the operation.

'I am very confident that God orchestrated this whole series of events, so that I would get to the right people who could take care of me. It took a lot of prayers and three or more miracles that would, in his time, bring healing, but each time, God was able to set us on new paths when before us had lain seemingly "desert" ground.'

'And we know that in all things God
works for the good of those who love him,
who have been called according to his purpose.'
Romans 8:28

In 1979 Miriam Perry was diagnosed as having systemic

lupus erythematosus. Hers was a three-pronged illness with symptoms in the areas of collagen, the immune system and a form of arthritic disease affecting the entire body. She explains,

'My muscles and joints, all the body tissues and organs, including my brain, heart and lungs were affected. The best way to describe my symptoms is to say that I felt like I had a very bad flu with a fever for over three and a half years. My skin could not be exposed to the sunlight for even fifteen minutes without severe pain. My stomach revolted every time I ate, because there was pain as the muscles needed to digest my food tried to do their work. My lungs stopped functioning at times, leaving me without a next breath, and my heart raced uncontrollably, leaving me exhausted. Besides these physical symptoms, I suffered from depression and an emptiness in my emotions that was truly the depth of my darkness.

'During this time God taught me from his Word that every one of us is dependent on him for everything: life, the very air that makes it possible for our lungs to take a next breath, our whole being. As I lay on my bed, he taught me that he loved me and delighted in me. I mattered to him – I, not my works.

'On 16 March 1983, my pastor called for a healing service for me at church. When I saw the announcement, I knew I wanted to be there. It was my 40th birthday, and I believe God gives birthday gifts. God gave me confidence that he would act through this service. Expectation is a part of the healing process.

'As the service of prayer for healing began, I, and a number of others, came up to the altar area. I walked with what was jokingly called the "Perry shuffle". I needed assistance with the two steps to the altar. Then, as we knelt, the pastor prayed general prayers and laid his hands on us, anointing one after another of us with oil and prayer. I had not knelt at the altar for several years because of the pain level. Now I was determined to kneel, though I almost passed out from the intense pain. After the pastor had laid hands on me and prayed and anointed me with oil, and moved on to the next person, I felt no different. The pain was just as intense. I wondered if I had understood God correctly. I could do nothing to make the situation different. It was in the hands of God. I believed, but that wasn't enough. "Help thou my unbelief", I cried with that biblical father.

'The pastor finished the prayers and excused us all. The person next to me offered to help me back down the steps. To this I responded in my pain, "No, I'm healed." With that fearful declaration of obedient faith I immediately felt a powerful surge of strength flow into my body.

'I leapt down those two steps and sat down beside my son Chris. Then I shouted: "Praise God! I'm healed! I've got to do that again." So I ran up the steps and down again. By this time the reality of what had happened flooded my whole being and I was filled with tears of joy. The service ended and my friends in attendance praised God with me. Afterwards, I challenged Chris to a foot race to the car. I beat him. Just imagine, thirty minutes earlier I could only shuffle my legs because my hips would not move, but now I could beat my 10-year-old son in a fifty-yard dash. I was healed. My heart has no damage from the rheumatic fever which I had at the age of twelve. I have no symptoms of arthritis. There is no trace of lupus in my blood.

'The initial response of the doctors was sceptical. Now they say that I have a "good remission" since there is no cure for systemic lupus, and final complications invariably lead to death. At first they did yearly ECGs on my heart, which had had damage since the age of 12, to verify my improved health, as well as blood tests. Now they do the routine tests and rarely even mention the lupus; I assume because they have decided that I am cured. You know, sixteen years of perfect health results tend to convince even the sceptical.

'I have put my hand in the hand of my God and your God, even Jesus Christ, the Great Physician, and I see his power at work every day.'

Today Miriam engages in full-time ministry.

'Therefore, if anyone is in Christ, he is a new creation; the old has gone, the new has come!'

2 Corinthians 5:17

Chapter 7

Tragedy to Triumph

'And the God of all grace, who called you to his eternal glory in Christ, after you have suffered a little while, will himself restore you and make you strong, firm and steadfast.'

1 Peter 5:10, 11

The pain and turmoil caused when tragedy strikes can often leave a heap of unanswered questions. Becoming debilitated as a result of an accident or life-changing incident draws out all the emotions of pain and despair as the victim grapples with the reality of a permanently changed life.

There are a number of characters in the Bible whose life stories depict the struggles experienced from tragedy to triumph. Joseph – betrayed by his brothers, sold into slavery, framed by a woman, sentenced to prison – from prisoner to prime minister. Moses – from discouragement to deliverer. Daniel – from captive to counsellor. Job – from victim to victor. Paul – from persecutor to preacher. In all accounts God turned the tables of events. From degredation each was raised to a position which enabled him to serve God more effectively.

Doris Bebe, at the youthful age of 21, received an injury that would change the rest of her life. A change, however, that would eventually lead from tragedy to triumph. Her story is a testimony to the power of God, even though it began with an encounter with the enemy.

'I started my high school year as most girls do, thinking of all the boys I would meet and which one I would love. I wanted to grow up fast. I had already made mistakes; I had begun to hang around a group in school who listened to heavy metal, singing songs like 'Shout at the devil', and going to concerts that girls of 15 should not have been going to. I wore the Satan symbol; little did I know that it would affect my whole life. What I thought was just a cool thing to do had a significant meaning. Just being one of a bunch of teenagers doing what seemed to be cool at the time would play a big part later on in my life.

'One night at a birthday party I did the Ouija board and it said that I would die young in a car accident. That same year a friend and I went to a fortune-teller at a flea market and she said the same thing. Some five years later, a lady in a bar read my palm and all of a sudden she threw my hand away. I could not get her to tell me what it said, but she told my friend, who in turn told me. It was the same thing but that this time I was going to die in a car crash at the age of 21. Well, at that time I was around nineteen so I felt I had plenty of time!

'Three months before my 21st birthday I moved back home to my parents. I thought that the second I turned 21 it would happen.

'My 21st birthday was 9 September 1989, and on 7 October at around 2:30am my life changed – almost a month to the day after my 21st birthday. I was having a roadside meal with a friend. We had just finished eating in the truck and the last thing that I remember was that I was putting the trash in the bag. Most of the rest of my story is based on what I was told by my friends and my grandmother because I have no memory of any of it.

'A young girl of 18 or 19 had been drinking at a local bar. When she was ready to leave, her friends tried to get her to stay and not drive. I was told she got in her car and drove away at high speed, something in the region of 85 miles an hour. She hit us head on. We were travelling around 40-45 miles an hour. I did not have a seat belt on and I was sitting in the middle. I was told that it was a very bad accident. There were four of us in the wreck. I was the worst injured and had to be cut out of the truck.

'They tried to do what they could for me but my injury was so great they needed to send me to a trauma hospital. The injury on my face was great. My cheek was pealed down and at that time they had to sew up my face without any pain relief, owing to the fact they did not know how bad my other injuries were. I was told that I yelled, screamed and cried very loudly.

'The emergency room staff told my friends and family that they had never seen anyone so badly injured survive. They moved me to a room and screwed a halo brace on me. This is a device that screws into your skull and is attached in four places, two in your forehead and two at the back. My neck was broken in the area where most folks similarly injured die – C-1 and C-2.

'My first memory when I woke up was of a group of people around my bed praying! I did not know who they were because no one I knew prayed!

Apparently my friends and family had called for a minister who brought other church members to the hospital to pray.

'I believe God answered the prayers of those willing to come and pray for me, a stranger. They didn't know me, but God did! And he had a plan for my life. I made it home from hospital about fifteen days later. I had a brain concussion, a broken neck, and plastic surgery on my face. I also had bruising to my mouth. I had lost half of one of my eyebrows and I had this crazy brace that went all the way down past my waist. Despite all this I did not feel any pain. I believe that Jesus bore the pain during this time.

'I wish I could tell you that I was grateful for my life and the fact that I could walk, but the truth was that I was angry, very angry. I did not understand at the time why this was happening. Yet God saved me from death and from being in a wheelchair. No one would believe that I had broken my neck.

'All my life I had lived across the street from a young man who had broken his neck after falling from a trampoline. I should have been very grateful, but instead I was very bitter towards God. I knew he had saved me, but I was angry that he let me live messed up as I was.

'I felt as though my life was ruined. I had had a face with no scars, and perfect teeth. I had never even had pimples! Now had I lost part of a front tooth, I had big steel bolts coming out of my head, and when I went out in public people stared. I wish I could say that I felt blessed to be alive, but I just wanted to die.

'I was young and selfish. I think, during that time, that God tried to speak to me, but I wouldn't listen. I turned him away and went on a road far worse than before. I became cold and bitter, and began to drink in an attempt to soothe the pain. While all this was going on, though, God never left me but attempted to reach me in ways too numerous to mention here. He allowed me to make mistakes as I searched for love and acceptance on my own terms. Then he gently pointed me towards the road I am on today.

'I'm so glad he never gave up, but continued to speak to me. I became a very tough person and he still has his work cut out to soften me up. But I really do want to thank God for the journey he has taken me on. It has been an interesting one! And I'm so grateful for the things he has allowed to touch my life. I will shout and tell the world of all he has brought me through!'

Today Doris lives each day to the full. She is married and a mother of four, and has become an active member in her church fellowship. God taught her to enjoy what she has. Her prayer is simply to be used as a channel through which the love of God can flow to others.

'Though you have made me see troubles,
many and bitter, you will restore my life again;
from the depths of the earth you will again bring me up.
You will increase my honour and comfort me once again.'
Psalm 71:20, 21

Marie Asner believes that it was the persistent and fervent prayers of her mother that enabled her to be healed from the effects of an accident that could have ended a promising career before it had even started.

'My mother was a musician. Not just "a" musician, but a church organist, a teacher of piano, and keyboard player in a dance band. Somewhere between my conception and birth, my mother decided I was to be a musician, too. When I was born, I was taken by her to rehearsals, whether they were in a church or band setting, and I lay in my bassinet by the piano when she gave lessons.

'At the age of 3, I showed musical acuity by pounding out Hoagy Carmichael's "Old Buttermilk Sky" with both hands. My parents were proud and sure I was going to be a musician of worth.

'The unexpected happened when I was 5. Before I could begin formal lessons, my left hand and thumb were crushed when a car door closed on them. The wind blew the car door shut while I was trying to climb on to the back seat. Searing pain ran from my fingertips to my elbow. I screamed and screamed. Someone wrapped a cold compress around my hand and I was hurriedly taken to the nearest hospital. My mother alternated between crying, "Why, Lord, why?" to repeating, "Have faith, have faith." When we arrived in the hospital parking lot, she closed her eyes, raised her face skyward and then, clasping my hand gently between her own hands, said said, "Hear my prayer, Lord."

'Through my pain at the hospital, I could hear doctors speaking to my parents. "Her hand is crushed and her thumb will probably never be moveable. It will be frozen in place. There is nothing we can do except put the hand in a cast. She is right-handed and will go through life fine."

'This was not acceptable to my mother. She phoned our minister from the hospital, plus her friends, and asked them to call *their* friends. Everyone was to pray for my hand to heal so I could be a keyboard musician for the Lord.

'My left hand was in a cast for six weeks. I managed well with my right hand and didn't miss playing the piano at all. At times when I came into the kitchen, I caught my mother in silent prayer and would tiptoe away, not quite sure what to do.

'It was time to remove the cast. Freed from the heavy plaster, I wiggled all my fingers, including the thumb, which to me seemed normal. The doctors had surprised expressions on their faces and one actually sat down rather quickly on seeing the new x-ray. My mother was elated. The x-ray showed a thumb joint that was clearly not aligned and should not be "the opposing thumb" at all. However, I was soon using my hand and began to practise the piano and take formal lessons.

'In the years that followed, I could not be a concert pianist, but I became a church organist, accompanist and piano teacher. The power of prayer healed my hand and allowed me to become a church musician. God has changed my life from potential tragedy to jubilant triumph.'

Today Marie has just retired from being an organist after forty years of service. Her left hand still doesn't 'look normal' but it obviously hasn't held her back in the least. That day in the hospital parking lot God heard and answered her mother's prayer.

Barbra adopted an attitude of thankfulness, acknowledging God's power to protect amid near-death experiences. She recalls the life-threatening experience of her daughter:

'At the age of 15 Kathleen was too young to date seriously, but she had a boyfriend. One evening, when I was leaving to pick up my son Paul from baseball practice, she asked if she could just go with her boyfriend to pick up his little brother from a friend's house. She said they would come right back. I said, "All right, just make sure you wear your seat belt, and come right home."

'It was my father's birthday and my younger daughter, Therese, was already at my father's house, waiting for us to come over with the cake I had yet to pick up from the store. I left to collect Paul from school, but decided to take the highway rather than the shortcut along the back roads.

'After leaving the school, Paul and I ran into the store for the cake and some last-minute goodies. As we were getting back into the car, we heard and saw paramedics, fire trucks, three ambulances and a multitude of police cars. I got a sick feeling in my stomach and said to Paul, "Somebody needs our prayers, quick." I wondered if there was a fire or a bad car accident. At one of the intersections I had to stop to let more emergency vehicles through, and

I prayed, "Lord, those people need you right now. Go to them and place your protective hand over them."

'We stopped at my parents' to drop off the food, before going home to pick up Kathleen, but my father met me at the car and told us to delay the party because Therese had fallen asleep. "Which way did you go to the school?" he asked. "There was a bad accident on the back road. I heard someone was killed. It happened just about the time you had to pick up Paul at the school and I know you always go that way. I was so happy to see you pull in. I had a gut feeling it was you."

'As Paul and I drove the short distance home, I could see our house was dark, and when Kathleen is home alone, she always burns every light. As I turned off the ignition, tears fell. "It was Kathleen," I told Paul. "I know it." I ran into the house and checked our answering machine; no one had called. I breathed a sigh of relief, thinking that someone would have called by then. "Paranoid", that's what they always called me, and that's what I was telling myself, "You're just paranoid!" Then the phone rang. It was the mother of Kathleen's friend, who worked in the emergency room of our local hospital. She told me that the three of them had been in an accident and were being taken to the hospital.

'I didn't call my husband at work, nor my parents. Paul and I just left for the hospital. As I pulled into the parking lot, one of the paramedics, someone we have known for years, met us at our car, tears streaming down his face.

'The next thing I remember was talking to the doctor in the hallway of the emergency room. He asked me if I believed in God, and with that my knees gave way. "No," he said quickly, "you don't understand. Do you believe in divine intervention?" I stammered a weak, "Yes", while not having a clue what he was talking about. He smiled at me and asked, "Do you know what shirt your daughter was wearing tonight?" Then he told me to go down the hall and look. "Your daughter is blessed with angels and so are you. From what the emergency personnel told me, there is no way that your daughter should be alive, let alone only have a few scratches."

'Kathleen was lying on a bed, waiting for more x-rays. When I got to her, we both sobbed. As I was hugging her I checked her shirt. After unzipping her jacket, I read the words, "Jesus Saves". I knew then what the doctor had meant. All three were treated and released. On the way home that night, Kathleen told me the story:

' "It was really weird, but about a quarter of a mile before the accident, I said, 'Wait. We forgot to put on our seat belts; my mother will kill me.' Then a car was coming towards us in our lane. He swerved, and I knew we had been hit on the passenger side of the car, where I was sitting. We got hit a total of three times because the car kept spinning in a circle. I felt a hand on my shoulder, holding me tightly in place. But, Mum, after it was all over, I could still feel a hand on my shoulder. I looked, but my boyfriend and his little brother had flown out the back window of the car, as we later found out, on the first spin. It was an angel, Mum, I know it!" I knew it too, especially when we went the next day to look at the car. It had been split in half, right underneath my daughter's seat.

'Witnesses said that the driver of the other car had been travelling at 90-95mph, and the point of impact at that speed was directly on Kathleen's door. The police report stated that the car door was found fifty feet away from the scene of the accident, with the seat belt attached. So, when the door broke loose, "the hand" was the only thing that saved my daughter's life.

'The Lord knew long before I did that my child was in trouble, and I will always praise him for saving her life and restoring mine.'

***'For he shall give his angels charge over thee,
to keep thee in all thy ways.'***

Psalm 91:11, KJV

Chapter 8

From victim to victor

'Now to him who is able to do immeasurably more than all we ask or imagine, according to his power that is at work within us, to him be glory.'

Ephesians 3:20, 21

He had been a victim of his circumstances since birth. He had always believed, as he had been told, that his blindness was a direct result of sin. Since birth, every day he lived with the constant reminder that he was paying the penalty for something he or maybe his parents had done. When Jesus was confronted with the question of who was at fault, he had taken the opportunity to dispel their narrow biblical reasoning and had explained, 'This happened so that the work of God might be displayed in his life' (John 9:3).

All healing is a demonstration of God's power displayed in the life. It is God to whom the glory and honour must be returned. Healing ought to draw men's attention to the healer rather than the healed. It is for God's purpose, for his name to be ultimately magnified, that such miracles are allowed to take place.

Jesus sought to release the blind man from both the spiritual and physical darkness in which he had been plunged. ' "Go," he told him, "wash in the Pool of Siloam." So the man went and washed, and came home seeing' (v.7). His testimony? ' "One thing I do know: I was blind but now I see!" ' (v.25). 'I was a victim trapped in a world of spiritual and physical darkness but now I have received victory from the Light of the World.'

Sharon Bailey was also a victim. She sat in the doctor's office, shocked. She had just come in for a routine check-up. Of course, she knew about the lump, but hadn't worried about it. After all, she was only 32 years old and healthy. The word 'cancer' had never occurred to her. Before the week was out, she was immersed in the world of the cancer victim.

'Victim. I hated that word, too. One afternoon as a team of doctors bombarded me with treatment options, I asked them to leave. In the quiet of that small sterile room, I began to talk to my best friend and Saviour. "You've always been there for me," I whispered. "I know this time it will be no different. But I need you now more than I've ever needed you before." His peace flooded the room and I called the doctors back in, ready to face what would come.

'That peace was a constant through the next few days. The news continually got worse. Not only did I have breast cancer, but also the tumour had spread to my lymph nodes. I felt as if I were on the outside looking in as they rolled me from room to room to a new set of needles and tests. One test revealed an ominous shadow on my brain. That night the doctors filed into my hospital room. Their faces were sombre. They spoke in whispers as if it would soften the news. My statistics of survival were rapidly going down. If this shadow proved to be cancer, my chance of surviving five years had just plummeted from 40 per cent to 10 – even after radical surgery, chemotherapy and radiation.

'They left the room and my husband and I sat wrapped in our grief. My children were young. I watched my husband as he wrestled with the news. I felt it was important that I share my wishes with him. The doctors had not been able to promise I would emerge unscathed from surgery on my brain. The shadow loomed over my central vortex—home to my memory, sight, and those abilities that make you who you are. As I began to tell him things about our children, our finances, my funeral, he closed his eyes. He stood and picked up my worn Bible and opened it to 2 Corinthians 4:7 and began to speak the words over me.

'"But we have this treasure in jars of clay to show that this all-surpassing power is from God and not from us. We are hard pressed on every side, but not crushed; perplexed, but not in despair; persecuted, but not abandoned; struck down, but not destroyed."'

'As he read, the words began to penetrate. I closed my eyes and silently began to worship the One who was bigger than I, bigger than cancer. My husband began to weep and worship God. The Spirit of God filled our room and we praised him for hours, singing and crying and even smiling at the tangible presence that filled the room Nurses, who knew the news we had just received, tiptoed in and then back out, not understanding, but respecting our time alone with God. Hours later, I fell into a deep, peaceful sleep.

'The next morning they wheeled me down the hall. They wanted to get a clearer picture of the shadow they had seen the day before. "It will only take thirty minutes," they said. Two hours later I was still confined in the metal tube. My husband was in the room with me; his only contact my bare feet sticking out of the tube. But I would hear him – still praising God as the MRI took pictures of my brain.

'Hours later I was surrounded by my family and many from my church. A doctor rushed in, still in his street clothes. "It's clear!" he shouted. "It's gone." My husband slid down the wall and began to weep while we celebrated. It was the first of many miracles over the next year.

'I fought against my family, believing that if God performed a miracle I would not need treatment. In the end *they* won, and I fought against anger the day I sat in the vinyl chair, waiting for the nurse slip the needle in my vein. The Lord spoke to me and asked me to trust him. "Let them know you are the One who healed me," I prayed. The nurses told me what I was to expect: nausea, hair loss, weakness, weight loss. The list went on.

'I felt the toxins hit my system and watched as my skin paled. I began to pray. "Help me make it through this hour," I said. Each hour, I prayed again. That night I went home and continued to pray, not stopping for the next nine months as I went through chemotherapy and radiation. The doctors were amazed each week when I walked through their door, my long hair intact. I never shed a pound; in fact I gained. I went back to work because I was not sick and soon became bored staying at home while members of my family were in school or at work. Each week I sat in the chair, surrounded by others who struggled against the devastating effects of chemotherapy, and prayed for them, my long, curly hair that reached below my shoulders a reminder that God was in the house. I could always see the chemotherapy hit my system. Within an hour my skin would be almost see-through. My veins on my chest and arms looked like slender blue rope, yet I did not feel anything.

'It seemed as if God revealed himself daily in small ways, but often in major ways. My family knew I was in God's hands and that they were seeing a miracle in progress. I worked each day and on Fridays only a half day, going to my weekly chemotherapy session. I was a youth sponsor in my church and many times I would go to a Friday youth retreat or fun night only hours after my treatment. With my hand bandaged, I would play volleyball with the teenagers. Several of the teens had promised to shave their heads if I lost my hair. They praised God with me when they realised it was a promise they would not have to keep.

'One day the doctor's office called. I had gone in for my weekly lab work. My white blood cell count was low and my immune system at a dangerously low point. They told me to leave work and stay home. It was the flu season and exposure to the current strain of flu could take my life. That afternoon, as my children climbed off the school bus, I watched them straggle up the sidewalk, their faces flushed, their eyes heavy. They had the flu. I rocked, bathed, and ministered to my children until my husband came home. Within hours, he, too, was sick and running a high fever of 104. I called the doctor who asked me to come immediately to the hospital. I stayed home with my children, wrapped in the assurance that God was with me. I took care of my family for the next three days and never came down with the flu. It seems as if God had decided to be my immune system that week.'

It's been eight years, and Sharon tells us that she now walks five miles a day. She writes full-time and hopes to share the news that God is real; his mercy is true. She reflects, 'I think the biggest miracle is that I have never felt like a cancer patient. I believe I have been through a battle and there were many hurdles God brought me through, fighting fear, but overcoming the overwhelming odds.'

One day Sharon asked her doctor, 'When will you decide I am cured?' He shook his head. 'Remission is declared after five years, and a cure after ten. I decided you were out of my hands a long time ago,' he said. 'I have watched as patients whose cancer was much less invasive than yours lose the battle. I believe you were cured a very long time ago.'

'Because you have been my help, therefore in the shadow of your wings I will rejoice. My soul follows close behind you; your right hand upholds me.'
Psalm 63:7, 8, NKJV

In early March, 1998, when she felt the lump in her breast, Gail ignored it, and told God that this could not be so. She felt he had tested her in other ways, but not through health problems. She couldn't bring herself to tell anyone for fear of what she would be told. 'Perhaps if I ignore it, it will go away', she thought.

'I did, however, talk to God often,' she told us. 'I say "talked" but the conversation was one way. I told him it could not be happening, that he was making a mistake. This continued for a month. In early April, consumed with fear, I finally talked to two friends who had experienced breast problems. These conversations scared me into making an appointment with our family doctor, who examined me and ordered x-rays. She seemed to think that everything was all right. So, when I talked to God, it appeared he was doing what I wanted, because everything seemed fine. I still wasn't listening, and that is the most important part of prayer. After seeing my doctor, I told my family and some Christian friends about the lump. They all began praying with and for me.

'The results of the x-rays came back with the news that there was not one, but three tumours, suspicious in type. My doctor immediately referred me to a local surgeon.

That, of course, did not fit with my idea of God's planning. I told God that I couldn't do it; I didn't have enough faith.

'Instead of seeing a local surgeon, I fought with my health insurer to see a surgeon who specialised in breast tumour surgery. I am not usually one to fight for something I want, but, for some reason, for once I did. They finally approved it, but the doctor I chose could not see me until the end of the month.

'At the end of April I saw the specialist. He recommended immediate surgery, but I put it off until the end of June. About three days before the scheduled surgery, I hit bottom. Finally, with an open heart, I reached out to God, knowing that only he could do what was best, praying, "Let this cup pass from me." At that point, I experienced a burning in my breast, something not really explainable. I didn't put much trust in the physical reaction, but I did know that I had surrendered my will to him that night.

'On the day of the surgery, my husband took me to the radiologist's office to have a mammogram, an ultrasound, and have dye injected into the tumours so they could be more easily seen by the surgeon. After this process, I was to go to the hospital for the surgery. This should have taken about an hour. The nurse spent that hour using ultrasound, trying to find something in the breast that resembled what showed on the original x-rays. The radiologist finally came in to see if he could find anything. He found nothing. He tried to get fluid out of the "tumours", but with no result. This went on for two hours.

'I knew something was going on, because I could overhear the conversation between the nurse and the radiologist, but I didn't put two and two together. Finally, the operating team called, wanting to know where I was. My husband, waiting in the reception room, heard the technician and the radiologist talking to the surgeon.

'I was told to get dressed and that the radiologist wanted to talk to my husband and me. We were ushered into a room where there were three sets of x-rays on the screens, which the radiologist used to demonstrate the difference between normal breast tissue and what a tumour looks like. He showed us the tumours in the first two x-rays and then what he considered a normal, healthy breast. All the x-rays were mine; the first two were earlier ones; the third was the current ultrasound. He could offer no explanation, but kept saying over and over that the tumours had been there and now they had gone.

'The surgeon still wanted to see all the ultrasound results for himself, and examine me, believing it to be an error. So my husband and I went to his office. I was still not sure what was going on. Could what the radiologist told us be true? The surgeon looked at the results and examined me. To his amazement, nothing could be felt in the breast or seen in the test results. God had removed this cup from me. All I could do was give him the glory and testify to his healing power.'

Gail was to learn important lessons that day. Even if she had only the faith of a mustard seed, God could work. It was clear beyond words that the only thing required of her was to trust him. It was also very clear that he doesn't need us to accomplish any of his purposes. He loves to hear and delights to answer the prayers of the saints on behalf of others.

'The Sovereign Lord is my strength;
he makes my feet like the feet of a deer,
he enables me to go on the heights.'

Habakkuk 3:19

For Jennifer Coyle it should have been the most joyous time of her life. She had just got married to her lifelong best friend. After their honeymoon weekend, Jennifer and her husband headed back home, happy but completely unaware of the crisis that loomed ahead.

'I noticed a twinge in my hip that seemed like a hot coil at certain times, like when sitting or leaning. I tried to exercise it out but each day I grew more and more uncomfortable. A visit to the local chiropractor revealed good news: "It's not a major problem like a herniated disc or nerve disorder. I think that with manipulation and old-fashioned walking you'll be fine." Relieved, I went to him faithfully but the pain was wearing me down. Then a friend insisted that I visit her orthopaedist and an MRI was ordered. I was shocked. The disc was severely herniated, my sciatic nerve was inflamed, and the doctor referred me to a neurologist. I couldn't stand, sit or walk comfortably, and was nauseated by the pain a great deal of the time. My husband told me he was praying for me.

'"It would be better to find a cure," I sobbed one night. "I'm exhausted, sick all the time, and maybe bedfast forever. If you want to leave me, I understand," and I cried my heart out. He took my hand and said we were in this together, for whatever was to be, and that prayer is essential in healing. Relieved that he was there for me, I didn't want to tell him that my spiritual life felt absent and that I just couldn't pray with him.

'Weeks of agony and sleeplessness wore me down; exercises and pain medication weren't bringing any noticeable change. The doctor recommended surgery the day I was rushed by ambulance to the local hospital after a bout of crushing pain left me gulping down air.

'My husband, my friend, who for weeks had slept on the

floor next to me in the living room, and had whistled and sung as though he were holding up just fine, had never shown me his terrified side, but he just could not imagine life without his active, vibrant new wife, who loved to wade the rivers fishing, take long walks and enjoyed nature as much as he did. He prayed to Jesus fervently, asking him to relieve my pain but also to bring me to God. He held my hand in the hospital as the nurse administered a strong and painful dose of pain medication. He asked me to pray with him and, because I was too beaten down to object, I closed my eyes and asked God, "Where are you? Don't you love me anymore?" Tears flowed as the emptiness and pain subsided and melted into a calm sleep.

'Two days before surgery, I noticed a definite improvement. During an excited call to the surgeon, I was urged to come in. Almost taken aback himself, he admitted that I seemed to be healing to some degree, and he said the magic words: "Let's postpone the surgery; we'll see how you are in two weeks' time." I went into the vacant ladies' room, dropped to my knees (not an easy stance at that time), and talked to Y'shua (God), my eternal friend, "Thank you and praise be to you! I know you wanted me to come to you after I thought I could do everything myself. I see the miracle, I thank you and I will never stop thanking you, and telling others about your powerful love." '

On 12 April 1998, Jennifer gave her heart to Christ, and was baptised in her local church. As the years have rolled along, she has enjoyed physical strength and activity. She is left with only a bit of numbness in her foot. It's a reminder that we are incomplete until we know God. It is our privilege to trust him with our very lives, and tell others about his healing power – a power that can transform us and give us victory in adversity.

Chapter 9

Free in Christ

'So if the Son sets you free, you will be free indeed.'
John 8:36

I am sure we can all relate to the apostle Paul when he says, in Romans 7:18-19: *'For I have the desire to do what is good, but I cannot carry it out. For what I do is not the good I want to do; no, the evil I do not want to do – this I keep on doing'.* The cycle is familiar to many sincere Christians: doing wrong, feeling the guilt and shame, being driven to repentance with a vow never to repeat the wrong and then succumbing once more to temptation. It's a cycle of spiritual bondage from which each Christian seeks to break free, but when we study the lives of the biblical characters we realise we're not alone. They all struggled with it.

Healing from this vicious cycle was what Paul sought when he came to the conclusion that in himself lay no power to contend with the selfish forces that emanated from within. His problem: 'What a wretched man I am!', was followed by the question: 'Who will rescue me from this body of death?' (7:24), and the remedy: 'Thanks be to God – through Jesus Christ our Lord!' (7:25). Then came the reappraisal: 'Therefore, there is now no condemnation for those who are in Christ Jesus, because through Christ

Jesus the law of the Spirit of life set me free from the law of sin and death' (8:1, 2).

God has done so much to make it possible for us to be free in Christ, free from the slavery of wrong habits and evil inclinations.

The powerful testimony of Don's compulsive disorder reveals how healing was achieved when he obtained freedom from the struggles and tensions in his mind.

'One October night in 1969 when I was working as a psychiatric nurse suddenly it was as if my mind snapped. I was overwhelmed by the thought that I might do physical harm to my children. Mixed with that irrational thought was the rational one, that as a psychiatric nurse I might be mentally ill myself. I was in the grip of what was then called Obsessive Compulsive Neurosis. The illness is now referred to as Obsessive Compulsive Disorder (OCD).'

OCD can take many different forms. Some people have the symptom of compulsive hand washing. Others feel the need to check things repeatedly, while others are continually filled with dread, simply because they feel they may have done something terribly wrong. And then there are those who are continually bombarded with repugnant thoughts totally alien to their nature, thoughts that can overwhelm and keep them on the brink of despair. Any of these symptoms can be totally exhausting.

Indeed, OCD has been described as the most torturing of mental illnesses. Having a mental illness, despite living in a supposedly enlightened age, is still not socially acceptable. This may be even more so in the Christian community than the secular. Many OCD people are fortunate in that they seem so 'normal'. Because they know they're sick, they're able to hide it. And all the time they're hiding, the suffering goes on. This was Don's experience.

'At the beginning of my illness, thirty years ago, the accepted treatment was psychotherapy, rest and medication, usually an anti-anxiety agent. I took a different approach. I did make three visits to a psychiatrist to confirm my self-diagnosis, but I had a family to support and felt I could not rest, and I couldn't afford perhaps years of psychotherapy.

'Rather than rest, I took on an even heavier schedule. I became active in my church and community, I worked hard at being a good husband and father – and I prayed. As never before in my life, I sought God's help. And with that my Christianity took on new meaning. I came to see that it's not just a religion, but also a way of life. But a cure didn't come overnight.

'The next year was an unending struggle. I pushed myself out of bed each morning, despite the depressed feeling that always hit at that time. I pulled myself through each day. Sometimes the thoughts would let up, only to come storming back. It's an amazing thing that my job performance never suffered. I can remember many hastily murmured prayers. followed by a feeling that God's angels were watching over me.

'Through all of this, I said nothing to my young wife. I was afraid she wouldn't understand. Had I been suffering from a physical illness, I would have shared my torment, but I was mentally ill – and having thoughts about harming my children. I understood my illness and knew I would never harm anyone, but how could she possibly understand? Might she not begin to fear me and decide to take our children and leave? I knew I could never withstand such a loss.

'And there was one other reason. What a terrible burden to dump on the person I loved the most! I could talk to no one but God.

'As time went on, I began to climb out of the deep pit into which I'd fallen. My self-devised treatment plan began to work. I still had my rough days and the morning depression was still there, waiting to snare me. But once I got going with my busy day, the depression would lift. It was rather ironic that while people were continually thanking me for helping them, I couldn't thank them for helping me. Not only were they helping, but I was gaining a love for my fellow humans I had never before possessed. I'd also come to one other conclusion: God's healing power is available to the mentally ill as well as the physically ill, but we need to pray as if it all depends on God, and work as if it all depends on us. Everyone will not be healed and I can't explain why – but the same rule applies nevertheless.

'By 1974, the thoughts were tormenting me much less frequently. I felt free for the first time in years. I'd fought my battle with my secret disease and with God's help, had won. I thanked him for his deliverance.

'I might have lived out the rest of my life without anyone knowing how sick I'd been, but suddenly, OCD, my bitter enemy, would reach out to ensnare me in a way I was totally unprepared for. It was as if Satan was trying a new approach. Dr Judith Rapoport's book, *The Boy Who Couldn't Stop Washing,* is the best I've ever read on OCD, says a propensity for the illness is inherited. She further states that the most likely progression will be from father to son.

'My second son, John, had been a happy little boy who grew into a very idealistic young man. At the age of 12, when other kids his age were engaged in pursuits of a trivial nature, John started a club to protect the environment. As a teen, when other kids were toting marijuana to school, John was carrying his Bible. While some teens were getting into trouble on Saturday nights, John was attending church activities. We were very proud when, during his senior year, he announced he wanted to attend a Bible College and go into full time Christian work, the first in our family ever to make such a commitment.

'When John graduated from college in 1982, things had never been better for my family. I seldom thought of the dark days of my illness. After graduation, John accepted a position with a Christian organisation. It was then that things started to go wrong for my son. Perhaps it was his idealism that worked against him. Things didn't turn out the way he expected. I could see he was stressed, but I knew I could do nothing but pray.

'I saw him become depressed, irritable and angry. To add to his career difficulties came difficulties in relationships with the opposite sex; they all turned sour. In conversations with him, I got a sense of total frustration. If all he wanted to do was serve God, why was his life in such chaos? The worst was yet to come.

'John quit working for the ministry and began taking jobs far below his intellectual capabilities. I wanted desperately to help him but didn't know how. Then one night he blurted out what was really bothering him. His words brought back all the horrible memories of 1969, only this time the pain was worse. My dear son was suffering the horror of Obsessive Compulsive Disorder. If at that moment I could have taken John's suffering upon myself, I would have gladly done so. But one thing I could not do – admit the truth about myself. My illness was now part of my past. I wanted it to stay there, buried forever. It was a decision I would come to regret. On that night I failed my family, my son and my God.

'I patiently explained to John that his thoughts were only that, thoughts; he needed to have no fear of acting on them. I told him about OCD, that it was a mental illness and was treatable.

'He went into therapy and for a while things seemed to get better. He even got a position with a foreign mission and was out of the country for a year. His letters home made no mention of OCD. I wanted to think that he had decided to treat his illness the same way I had, by being so busy he'd have no time for unwanted thoughts. I prayed fervently that that would be so.

'When John returned from his overseas mission, he was expecting to get a stateside assignment with the same organisation. During his initial interview, he had done what we had always told him to do – been honest. Now he was turned down because of his psychiatric history. It was a blow. It appeared that he was good enough for an overseas assignment, but not good enough for his own country. He came home while he decided what to do with his life.

'I would lie in bed at night and hear him crying out. My wife didn't understand, but I did. On Thanksgiving Day, 1987, John attempted suicide, and was admitted to a psychiatric hospital. I knew then that my well-kept secret would have to be revealed.

'For twenty years no one had known but God. When I told my wife, she held me tightly and cried. How foolish I'd been! I was married to a Christian wife who loved me.

'Why had I ever feared she wouldn't understand? Before the day was out, my entire family knew the truth. Our meeting brought tears, hugs and words of support. We were a family. We would now join together to help the one who needed it. John need have no fear of desertion. We held hands and prayed that John would be delivered.

'I was somewhat apprehensive about my meeting with John at the hospital. Would he be angry because I hadn't told him the truth? John explained that while he was angry about having OCD, he in no way blamed me, that I could not help having OCD any more than he could. With those words, a heavy burden was lifted from my shoulders.

'I had been carrying an unnecessary load of guilt. Parents want only to pass on good things to their child-ren. I had passed on a disease. But John was right. I couldn't help it. God knew it and John knew it. I guess it just took me a while.'

It's been twelve years since this occurrence. Both Don and his son John have struggled much, but John's now married with a family of his own. He has a good job in the secular world but is a faithful servant in his church. Don, who is busy enjoying his grandfather years, concludes, 'Life has been good to both of us.'

'But you, O Lord, are a compassionate and gracious God, slow to anger, abounding in love and faithfulness. Turn to me and have mercy on me; grant your strength to your servant and save the son of your maidservant.'

Psalm 86:15, 16

For most of Vivienne Tsouris' life, she, too, had struggled with unreasonable compulsions.

'As a child I was compelled to do things in certain numbers. For example, if I blinked I was obliged to blink four times, or if I knocked my ankle I would have to make sure that the correct number of subsequent knocks was administered. Thoughts also needed to be brought into line, so that even after performing particular strange actions the required number of times I invariably had to repeat the whole sequence until I was able to think simultaneously the correct thoughts. All this without anybody noticing, of course!

'By the time I was married with a young family, constant hand-washing had become a major part of my routine. The rules were endless, but dead secret. If I awoke in the night I would creep around the children's bedrooms, touching each one on the forehead, feeling like a ghost gliding about on its habitual nocturnal haunts. But always the hardest part was getting through the bedroom door afterwards, stepping backwards and forwards through the opening as I endeavoured to control my erratic thoughts. Of course, there were long periods of time when the compulsions became fewer, and my habits became so much a part of everyday life that I scarcely noticed them. But during times of anxiety or insecurity my obsessions became unbearable. Prayer brought no real relief, and I was convinced that this was just an unavoidable part of my make-up.

'After the death of my parents I found my mind being taken over to an alarming degree. There were constant voices in my head, which often felt like a battleground. I couldn't help wondering if there might possibly be a way out of my obsessive behaviour, if only I could find it.

'One night as I lay in bed I was intrigued by a persistent mental picture which seemed to impress itself upon me. The image was a part of the inside of my brain, and there, attaching itself to the intricate convolutions, was a cancer. As I focused in on the vision I sensed God communicating some fascinating truths.

'As cancer cells tend to imitate and take on the form of the normal cells of whichever organ they are invading, so the obsessive compulsive disorder which I had been host to for so long had developed alongside of me. It had so successfully integrated itself within my personality and lifestyle that I had come to accept that this was simply the way I was. What God revealed to me in that instant, however, was that the disorder was a foreign entity and did not belong there. I prayed, not very hopefully, for further help, and eventually fell asleep.

'Because of the deep sense of peace instilled within me by this experience, I decided that instead of engaging in my usual morning prayer time I would just sit quietly and meditate for a while, listening to the Holy Spirit. Two scriptures came strongly to mind. Firstly, John 16:13, KJV: "When he, the Spirit of truth, is come, he will guide you into all truth." And secondly, John 8:32: "You shall know the truth, and the truth shall make you free." I remembered reading that if we ask the Holy Spirit to lead us to the truth and root cause of a problem, he will do so. I could believe this happened to other people – but to me? Well, I would try.

'A few minutes later I was reaching for a pen and paper in order to list the many memories, pictures and words which came flooding into my consciousness. It occurred to me that as far back as I could remember I had had a sense of being surrounded by a number of tall white spiritual beings who had a desire to participate in my life.

'At this point, before relating any more of my experiences under the Holy Spirit's guidance, it is necessary for me to tell you that two years before I was born my mother gave birth prematurely to a baby boy who lived for just four hours. This experience left her with deep traumatic scars and an unutterable sense of regret that she had never been able to hold the child in her arms, for she had been denied any physical contact with him. My birthday, 28 March, was the date of the baby's burial two years earlier, a fact which would undoubtedly seem significant to a grieving mother.

'The list of dream-memories and associations which continued to flood my mind was seemingly endless. However, I eventually found myself puzzling over a vivid mental picture which, for a while, I couldn't quite make out. "What is it, Lord?" I asked, intrigued. The answer came in a flash of revelation. The image was a picture of a birth – my birth! The fragmented thoughts, images and memories began to merge together to form a picture. I had always sensed that in my mother's eyes I had been a replacement, and to some extent a measure of healing for the unresolved trauma. After losing the baby she had suffered several miscarriages and only succeeded in conceiving me with medical help. Obviously I was a much-wanted child.

'The picture suggested that even in the womb I had been affected by my mother's anxious concern. She was understandably prone to be over-protective, and so much so that she unwittingly invoked the intervention of spirit guides to take care of me, thinking that she was asking for the loving care of the spirit of my grandfather!

'Colossians 2:15 speaks of Christ, "having disarmed principalities and powers," or having "made a public spectacle of them, triumphing over them." (NKJV.) Obviously Christ's resurrection from the dead is the ultimate triumph over evil. Those who have received the gift of his life are made triumphant over demonic spirits. So, in response to this amazing revelation, I thanked God for my sure salvation through Christ. I asked forgiveness for having participated in a relationship with demonic powers, albeit unwittingly. I renounced that relationship and all communication with wrong spiritual influences, and in the name of Jesus Christ commanded those spirits to get out of my life.

'Only the Holy Spirit could expose and unravel such a tangle of relational cause and effect. And only the Lord Jesus could offer the solution.

'I realised that the power of Satan is in the lie, and in his ability to deceive. Once the lie is exposed our minds become free. I knew instantly that I had been released from mental bondage but, of course, the habits took longer to break. Every time I habitually touched something I would think, "I don't have to do this any more." The sense of freedom was exhilarating.

'During times of stress or anxiety I have to exert extra resolve to keep my mind free, but the unalterable fact is that the Holy Spirit led me to the truth which exposed Satan's deception.'

'You will know the truth
and the truth will set you free.'
John 8:32

Chapter 10

Peace of mind

'Nevertheless, I will bring health and healing . . . . I will heal my people and will let them enjoy abundant peace and security.'

Jeremiah 33:6

The relationship between mind and body is very intimate. When one is affected, the other sympathises. The condition of the mind has great influence on the well being of the body. Grief, anxiety, discontent, remorse and guilt tend to break down the life forces and physically decay the body. By contrast, contentment, thankfulness, joy, love and trust aid in strengthening the soul. It was Solomon who said, *'A cheerful heart is good medicine, but a crushed spirit dries up the bones'* (Prov. 17:22) .

Such abiding peace and rest of spirit have but one source. It was of this that Christ spoke when he said, *' "Come to me, all you who are weary and burdened, and I will give you rest" '*(Matt. 11:28, 29). *' "Peace I leave with you; my peace I give you. I do not give to you as the world gives. Do not let your hearts be troubled and do not be afraid" '* (John 14:27).

Job is an example of one who had such peace of mind. Even though he had lost all and suffered severe boils, he was able to say, *'The Lord gave and the Lord has taken away; may the name of the Lord be praised'* (Job 1:21). There was no assurance that he would be healed, but because he was secure in his trust in God he was prepared to face the future with complete acceptance of his condition. *'Though he slay me, yet will I hope in him'* (Job 13:15).

It was for mental restoration that Irene Carloni prayed when, at the age of 17, her son Mike, with his whole life ahead of him, was diagnosed with Multiple Sclerosis (MS). A once happy and contented child had become an unhappy, angry and rebellious teenager. Irene tells the story.

'My husband and I, along with our doctors, looked at many research programmes that treated MS. Mike even participated in one research programme at the local university. We prayed for physical healing for Mike and even looked to our church for help. We went to several healing services but never saw any improvement. During this time I shed many tears. In my sorrow I found myself thinking about Mary, the mother of Jesus. How did she feel when she saw her Son suffering? It was all too hard to understand.

'The years slipped by while I continued to pray for Mike's healing. Meanwhile, Mike's anger and rebellious attitude continued to grow worse. I found that I was also becoming more impatient and short-tempered. One day during my prayers, I was prompted to give my son to the Lord.

'"Lord, I know you're in control of everything. I give you my son and I will accept whatever you decide to do with his life. Please help me to accept his illness and have enough patience to care for him."

'After praying, I experienced a feeling of peace which allowed me to see Mike in a different light. When Mike was angry I made jokes and sang silly songs instead of becoming angry myself. Gradually Mike's anger slipped away. My husband noticed that Mike was happier and more content. In time, our daily lives settled into a pleasant routine.

'We asked the doctor about the change in Mike's personality. He told us that MS had affected Mike's memory and left him with a feeling of wellbeing. Secretly I smiled to myself. I knew that this was a healing from the Lord and an answer to my prayers. The Lord had healed Mike in his own way, and healed me as well.

'Twenty-three years have passed since Mike was diagnosed with MS. Through God's healing, our anger turned to laughter and frustration turned to peace.

'You have turned for me my mourning into dancing;
You have put off my sackcloth and
clothed me with gladness, . . . O Lord my God,
I will give thanks to you for ever'.

Psalm 30:11, 12, NKJV

As Joan began her first day teaching a new class, little did she know that one of her pupils, whose psychological disorder seemed disruptive, would bring out all her patience and love to see him through.

'I thought he was just trying to clear his throat. But when he was still "barking" at the end of the first school day, I realised I was in for trouble. The "ark-arking" every two or three minutes was a distraction, to say the least. To compound the problem, the facial tics and contortions Benny manifested brought giggles and interruptions from the class all day long.

'On the second day of school I was prepared, I thought. I had anticipated every move and would be equal to the task. I would seat Benny adjacent to my desk away from the other students. This would put him at a disadvantage, being so far from the chalkboard, but I reasoned I could give him lots of individual help.

'It was a disaster! The constant "ark-ark" forced me to repeat instructions continually. Moving Benny away from the other children seemed only to make his barking louder.

' "Teacher, I can't hear. What did you say to do?" the children asked repeatedly.

'When the second day of school ended, I rushed to the counsellor's room in desperation. I learned a lot from Benny's psychological report from the year before. He had "alcohol foetal syndrome". There was no prenatal nutrition, plus unsuccessful attempts at abortion. Benny was abandoned at birth. He was being reared by a caring grandmother who had done everything she could to change her grandson's barking and facial contorting. The psychologist's findings included the beginnings of Tourette's syndrome. The disease begins with facial contortions and tics.

' "Lord, I need help with Benny," I prayed every night. For the first time in twenty years of teaching I didn't know what to do or how to cope with this kind of situation. I prayed for wisdom daily. I knew the child had suffered from malnutrition, rejection and defeat, so I resolved to bombard him with prayer, love and supportive individual instruction.

'Being a public schoolteacher, I could not pray out loud, but I could pray mentally and silently in the Spirit. In my mind I warred daily for Benny. The more I prayed, the worse Benny seemed to get. One day I was trying to teach the regrouping concept in maths. The children were having a hard time grasping it, and the constant "ark-ark" from Benny made teaching almost impossible. Then a remarkable thing happened.

'I was standing before the class when I found myself saying: "Benny, come up here please." He came and stood beside me and I resumed teaching. He resumed 'ark-arking.'

'I put my hand on Benny's shoulder and silently prayed for him while teaching maths at the same time. In the weeks and months that followed, the same scene happened many times. Benny would bark, and I would stand him by me with my hand on his shoulder, teaching out loud, but praying for him silently. I was patient and obedient in what I perceived the Lord would have me do. I knew children need reassurance, but I just didn't realise that my hand on Benny's shoulder was a touch he needed.

'Occasionally, I would pat his shoulder and that, along with prayer, was moving the mountain in Benny's life.

'Changes were so gradual that I hardly noticed them. I had either learned to live with the "arking", or it had disappeared so gradually that I had become accustomed to the silence! Until one day in March one of my students exclaimed before the whole class: "Teacher, have you noticed that Benny doesn't bark any more?"

'And then it hit me! "That's right! I can't remember the last time I heard Benny bark. Hallelujah! Thank you, Lord!" I was even more ecstatic when a copy of Benny's latest psychological appraisal was given to me.

' "A very definite improvement," the report read. "I don't know what you're doing," the counsellor had written, "but keep it up – it's something very right."

'It has now been four years since Benny was in my room. I have kept up with his progress.

' "How's Benny doing?" I casually asked one of his teachers the other day. "Does he ever make funny noises or weird faces?"

' "No," she replied, "but he told me something very strange the other day."

' "What?" I asked anxiously.

'"Well," she said hesitatingly, "Benny says he doesn't bark any more."'

'Do not be anxious about anything, but in everything, by prayer and petition, with thanksgiving, present your requests to God. And the peace of God, which transcends all understanding, will guard your hearts and your minds in Christ Jesus.'

Philippians 4:6, 7

The story of 6-year-old Holly Godbehere (God-be-here) highlights the fact that low self-esteem can often contribute to destabilising peace of mind. Holly lived in the northwest suburbs of Chicago in a family of five. She came from a Christian family with a beautiful home, in a safe, quiet, tree-lined neighbourhood. The children, one boy and two girls, were active, along with their parents, in church and school activities. Holly was the youngest of the children, a little cutie with big china-blue eyes, fair skin and lots of freckles. Her sister Sally, who was three years older, was another beauty with chestnut brown hair, big brown eyes and a creamy olive skin. Holly just longed to have the flawless freckle-less complexion of her sister Sally.

As cute and sweet as Holly was, her freckles started to become a big problem to her. She hated those freckles and complained and cried about them almost every day. She felt she could never be pretty like her sister as long as she had those freckles. Holly's mother continues the story.

'Even our pastor had to be asked, gently, not to call her "freckle face" at church on Sunday mornings as she cried all the way home. I saw her sadness and she seemed so unhappy. Could a 6-year-old have depression, I wondered? It was ridiculous! We just couldn't seem to convince her that her freckles were not important; they didn't change who she really was; and that she was so special to us. But she didn't like them and she was angry!

'I didn't know what to do. I couldn't get rid of her freckles and it was getting to be too big a problem. Her schoolwork started to suffer and her teacher suggested a tutor to help her in reading. Well, I soon learned this was not just a passing fancy but a high priority item and I'd best get help the only place I knew to get it. I turned to the Lord and prayed every day that God would guide, direct and give me the wisdom to solve this problem that was beyond me. What to do and how to help my little girl feel good about herself. As her mother I could only let her know she was so very special to us.

'My prayers were very decidedly answered in no time at all. Within two weeks, we received a letter in the mail from a modelling agency. They wanted Holly for modelling. When I read the letter to her, she felt so very special and so good about herself. "My freckles aren't so bad after all. It's a shame Sally doesn't have any freckles." Two days after that, Holly came home from school, announcing she had won the United Way Poster Contest for her class and would be a special guest of honour at a dinner at a restaurant – and her father and I would be her guests! She was so proud.'

Prayers for this mother and her little girl were answered. Indicative of her surname 'God-be-here', God was certainly there for her. Holly was once again a happy beautiful little girl with a precious light sprinkling of cute little freckles. Her story reassures us of the precious promise in Isaiah 54:13, *'All your children shall be taught by the Lord, and great shall be the peace of your children.' (NKJV.)*

With physical healing it's easy to see tangible improvement. Harder are those inner wounds, the ones that come from tragedy and emotional pain. Brenda Nixon shared the healing of her father Joe's 'inner wounds', gained from the incessant memories of World War Two.

'In the 1940s our world was at war with itself. A 17-year-old American farm boy called Joe, to whom service was important, quit high school to enlist. When he was 19 he faced active combat with his platoon stationed in Okinawa, Japan. The horrors and atrocities no eyes should ever see left permanent scars on this young man.

'Following the close of World War II, he returned to his small farm safely nestled in the hills of southern Ohio. He was met, as were many, with a hero's welcome. Life to the returning solder was abundant with new possibilities and soon he found a job as a carpenter. A job God would use to bring healing.

'Years passed and Joe worked his way up to becoming a carpenter's foreman. His many responsibilities included hiring skilled carpenters for each job-site. The United States had enacted an Equal Opportunity law, mandating the hiring of minorities. Many were interviewed and hired by my father, who was noted for being a fair boss. But his most heart-wrenching decision, one that would change the direction of two lives, was to hire a Japanese veteran of World War II.

'Known as "George the Jap", Joe's new hire soon proved his worth. He was a dependable, conscientious, hard worker. The war years were far away and the emotional distance enabled the two to become acquainted. As they exchanged facts about their families and children, similarities brought them closer, so they shared stories about their childhood, then their war experiences. George admitted his inbred hatred for Americans who invaded his country. Joe confessed his feelings against the Japanese bombing of Pearl Harbour and horrid memories in Okinawa. The old wounds still caused pain, yet the two men found comfort in their friendship.

'As a flower unfolds, revealing its beauty, so a friendship between George and Joe began to unfold. One day George questioned Joe's belief in God. His response led to a discussion of spiritual matters. He witnessed to God's forgiveness soon after returning from war, of God's love and power to change lives, and he shared how prayer made it possible to forgive those he fought against.

'George showed an increasing hunger for God's grace and forgiveness. The pain that plagued the two men began to ease as things of eternal importance took their place. Joe prayed for George's salvation. He wanted George to know God's grace. Old wounds were healed but God's work wasn't finished.

'Suddenly and without warning, George was taken with a serious illness, his return to work improbable as his fragile life began slipping away. Their friendship now in full bloom, Joe visited George daily at the hospital where he witnessed to and prayed with him.

'From the hospital bed one day, George looked in the eyes of his American friend and asked to be led to Jesus. Gently, Joe guided George in the sinner's prayer where he experienced true freedom. Once mortal enemies, two old soldiers embraced in joy as God's work was complete. The old mental wounds were healed.'

'Do not conform any longer to the pattern of this world, but be transformed by the renewing of your mind. Then you will be able to test and approve what God's will is – his good, pleasing and perfect will.'

Romans 12:2

Chapter 11

When hope hurts

'Trust in the Lord with all your heart
and lean not on your own understanding;
in all your ways acknowledge him,
and he will make your paths straight.
Do not be wise in your own eyes;
fear the Lord and shun evil.
This will bring health to your body
and nourishment to your bones.'

Proverbs 3:5-8

The apostle Paul's unanswered prayer for his 'thorn in the flesh' reminds us that prayers are not always answered according to our own will. Paul says, 'Three times I pleaded with the Lord to take it away from me. But he said to me, "My grace is sufficient for you, for my power is made perfect in weakness."' (2 Cor. 12:7-9)

Spiritual healing, a deeper reconciliation between God and man, is the highest and most complete form of healing one can receive. It's at times when God seemingly fails to act that in the midst of suffering God is calling us first to enter a spiritual renewal with him.

I realised this in a prominent way in 1998 when I was diagnosed with tuberculosis while pastoring in the city of Gloucester, England. I had contracted the illness via a medical laboratory dealing with infectious diseases. Although I prayed sincerely for healing, there was no immediate miraculous answer. The physical cure eventually came through the prescribed means given by the medical team. Indeed, God uses all means necessary for healing, including the conventional remedies prescribed by our doctors today.

However, it was while I was in hospital during the early stages of my illness that the Lord made me realise the absolute importance of total dependence on him. Pastoral ministry can often come with many pressures and self-defined expectations. It's very easy to become so absorbed in the work of spiritually watering the souls of others that your own spiritual well can run dry.

God was to show me during those days in hospital that *'the battle is not yours [mine], but God's'* (2 Chron. 20:15). Whereas I had become so immersed in my work, to the point that I began to feel indispensable to my church, the Lord lovingly reminded me to whom the church really belonged. I too was just an instrument, together with all the other members, and whether I was to be there or not, God's Church would still move forward.

I reaffirmed my commitment to being led by God rather than to leading, to waiting on him, and resting awhile if needs be, so that I could offer a more effective ministry, pleasing to God. My illness resulted in a healing far deeper and higher than the physical, for although I became cured of tuberculosis, I received a spiritual restoration that brought me a greater dependence on the awesomeness of God.

In like manner Carol Ballensky was to learn that although she couldn't put right the events of her past, she gained more than she bargained for when she experienced a fresh spiritual encounter with God.

'I instantly identified him when our eyes met in the lobby of my hotel. He was a handsome, well-educated businessman. His vivid blue eyes and dark hair gave him away; he looked exactly like my brother. On the way to dinner that night, I looked forward to catching up on the last sixteen years. At last I had met my dad!

'He had left my brother and me when I was two years of age. There were no memories to reflect on; I couldn't remember a thing about him. The only whisper from the past was a lingering desire and hope that someday he would come back and love me.

'By the time I had graduated from High School I could no longer stifle the desire to see him. After much agonising soul-searching, I called and asked if we could meet. My palms were sweating and my heart felt like a jackhammer, but he was receptive! He had established his home, business, and new family in the Hawaiian Islands.

'As we were seated for dinner at an exclusive Island Country Club, I sat viewing the deep green palms against the tropical orange sunset. The air was balmy, the breeze warm and soothing. I wanted the beauty of that moment to last forever. But the euphoric feeling was shattered in a moment. I looked at my father, but he didn't have to say a thing. The look in his eyes told me he had no desire or intention of starting a relationship, especially one of father to daughter. We sat listening to the ukulele and the band happily singing, and my heart felt as though it was breaking into a million little pieces. I wanted to cry. He was seeing me out of a sense of obligation, nothing more.

'I chose to hide my disappointment, but as I looked at him my frustration grew. All I could see was a man who appeared to be genuinely kind and generous. Why couldn't he accept me?

'Then, nearly twenty years after that first meeting, he actually agreed to meet me again. He had relocated to Las Vegas, only a few hours from my home. I was happily married and had two beautiful children of my own. My son and daughter were beginning to feel the absence of grandparents in their young lives. My only chance was to remind my father of a great and awesome God who could restore any relationship, including ours. I knew he had grown up in a Christian home. Family members assured me he had once professed to love God. I was ready to roll out the red carpet and invite him to be a long-awaited part of my life.

'I was not there to demand an explanation; I was offering complete forgiveness for his choice to leave me without a father. All I hoped for was a small beginning, even an inkling of interest in me and my children – the grandchildren he had never seen.

'I assumed our meeting would be brief and unemotional by the nature of his suggested meeting place, a smoke-filled, bell-ringing, clamouring, Vegas Casino. It couldn't get much more impersonal than that! But I had a mission. I felt the Lord calling me to make one last attempt at reconciliation. I had prayed about it, and knew the Lord was directing me to speak with my father, to share my story and my faith. I went with an open heart and an ocean of hope. I was sure he could find a place for me in his heart. It was risky, but God rewards the faithful; maybe my dad would change his mind.

'We could feel the tension rising as we made small talk and ordered lunch. Grasping for words, I stammered, "My family holidays near here every year; I've thought about calling and inviting you to spend a day boating with us – you could meet my kids; it's only an hour from Vegas." Instantly, I knew I had made a huge mistake. A look of horror fell across his face as he shook his head, saying, "Well, as you know, I am not very kid oriented. I hope you realise this isn't your fault but I can't look back.The past is too painful."

'It was then I realised; I really had come for an explanation. I felt my face contort as I tried not to cry. As the tears streamed down my cheeks, I forced a smile, "I really didn't expect anything different; I just had to try one more time." I knew then that anything I had ever wanted to say to him I'd better say in the next few minutes; I drew a deep breath. "Dad, I want you to know, even though I don't know you, that I love you because you're my father." His eyes narrowed in disbelief. "I want you to know what happened in my life, and how God has changed me."

'"As you know, Mum remarried after you left. The man she married was a child molester." Now his mouth hung open in shock. I wasn't sure whether to go on, but I had no choice other than to finish what I had started. "Because he was a deacon in our church everyone trusted him. He began molesting me when I was 5. I ran away when I was 14, and when they found me, they sent me to live with my grandparents because I revealed the ugly secret." I plunged on. "I spent my teenage and young adult years raging at the unfair world I was forced to live in. Dad, the first time we met, when you lived in Hawaii, I was a mess. I drank the whole time I was there. You saw the hurt child who hated the world; now my life is so different. After over ten years of self-destructive behaviour and running from the hurts of my past, I realised I needed professional help. With the assistance of a Christian counsellor I've begun the process of sorting out the tangled web of my past. I love the Lord and want to share with others the hope I've found. If it weren't for God I wouldn't be here today."

'As I shared my faith with him, I could see he wasn't buying it. I felt like I was talking to myself. Distracted, I sensed he was in a hurry to leave. I gathered my things to go, but left one thing behind – my hope. It hurt too much to hope. Was it so unreasonable to ask for the love of my own father?

'Gripping the steering wheel with one hand and wiping away stinging tears with the other, I drove back to my hotel. I was through hoping for things that would never happen. I had dreamed all my life of parents who would love me instead of hurting me. I had put my faith in God, been obedient to his prompting, and had sustained heart-wrenching rejection.

'I began crying out to God, "Why do I love this man who doesn't love me? He didn't even want to spend one hour talking with me. Why do I long for the attention of a family who don't care about me? Why does life have to hurt so much?" Then it was as if God was saying, "Carol, that's how much I loved you when you didn't love me back. I loved you when you didn't even want to spend one hour talking with me. I longed for you when you turned me away. The love you are feeling for your father, the pain you are feeling from his absence, is just a glimmer of what I feel for you, and the sorrow I experience in your absence."

'I thought, then, of a verse I had discovered just months before, "For my father and my mother have forsaken me, but the Lord will take me up" (Psalm 27:10, NAS). I was reminded that I have a heavenly Father who loves me more than any earthly father possibly could. I knew I must have hope to survive. For me, parental relationships have brought only despair, but Jesus promises never to leave, never to disappoint, and never to change.

'Jesus suffered unjust and undeserved rejection at the hands of people who should have loved him. He knows how I feel. He gives the hope of everlasting love, despite the pain caused by those who have chosen to hurt me.

'He gives me the opportunity to overcome rejection in my own life because I choose to place my trust in him. Yes, the hurts of the past still need to be acknowledged and grieved, but he promises to comfort me all along the way.

'I am confident that through Christ my heavenly Father loves me completely. I am a daughter of the King! He gives me new hope when hope hurts.'

'Be strong and take heart,
all you who hope in the Lord.'
Psalm 31:24

Sharon also had a hope. Her son Justin was born hydrocephalic. The diagnosis was 'vegetative state', but then the diagnosis was reversed. There was brain tissue. Suddenly, anything could happen. Far from being a 'vegetable', her son could be a 'normal child'.

Sharon recalls how she fell to the floor on her face, crying in her despair, 'God, is my lack of faith keeping you from performing a miracle on my own son?' The answer she got was straight from the Scriptures: *'By grace you have been saved, through faith . . . not from yourselves, it is a gift from God.' Eph. 2:8.*

Justin survived for four-and-a-half months instead of a few days, but in that short time Sharon was to learn that sometimes our vision of healing is not the only way God answers our prayers. Instead, he gave her an accepting and loving heart and spiritual healing. In our correspondence Sharon revealed, 'I had to ask God to forgive me for believing he was how I had been *taught* he was, and then I got to know him all over again *for who he really is.*'

Sharon's experience is a challenge to us all – to know God for who he really is and not for who we think he is.

'"You will seek me and find me when you seek me
with all your heart. I will be found by you,"
declares the Lord.'
Jeremiah 29:13-14

Ellen Bergh was another who was challenged to a greater understanding in her perception of God. Her story reveals the truth that God's thoughts are not always our thoughts, neither are his ways our ways. (See Isaiah 55:8.)

'In 1980, after ten years of marriage, I left my husband for someone else. The Lord.

'Our party lifestyle had brought me to the gates of insanity and death, until God tossed out a lifeline and I grabbed it. I announced my conversion to my husband Clarence as he worked filling out insurance forms on my latest trip to the mental ward. He shook his head, too shell-shocked to believe my news could make any difference. But God makes all the difference. My craving for escape into intoxication or death began to lift. I clung to God and avoided joining my husband in our old pastimes of alcohol and drugs.

'My recovery baffled him and he resented my new sober companions. I began to see my marriage as a run-down piece of property that ought to be abandoned. Focusing on all my husband's shortcomings, I prayed for God to change him. Over the next year and a half I launched an assault to convert this heathen. Deciding he was a captive audience in the bathroom, I left magazines and tracts. Over tea I shared my spiritual insights until his eyes glazed over. I became a pain to live with. Why couldn't he just get with it?

'When out to dinner, I nobly sipped my coke and watched with distaste as he ordered a beer to prove he didn't have a drinking problem. We had less and less in common since I was so spiritual and he a true vulgarian.

'One morning, as I whined to the Lord, I sensed him asking me, "Do you love me?"

'I was taken aback. "Of course I love you, Lord. You gave me a new life."

' "Would you do anything for me?"

' "Yes, Yes! Send me anywhere. What is it, Lord?"

'"Love your husband for me. I loved you while you cursed me. Will you do this for me?"

'Ashamed, I apologised and asked God to help me see my husband through his eyes. I'd fallen into such fault finding, I had to visualise a neon sign on my husband's head, flashing: "God's property, no tampering!" It would act as a caution light when I felt tempted to nag him. I prayed I would find things to praise Clarence about, and found them, to our mutual surprise. Trust grew in me through obedience to the Lord. I sensed a change was in the wind. God was preparing my husband for something. But what?

'A few months later, his mother was diagnosed with terminal cancer, and several times Clarence travelled to be by her bedside. He picked up her Bible, the same one she had read every morning of every visit to our home. He began to read, in the hope of comforting her as she drifted in and out of consciousness, and God used his faith, born out of hearing the Word he himself read to his mother. The Lord was to bring Clarence into a new life just as his mother slipped out of hers.

'Clarence began to receive the personal attention of his loving Heavenly Father, tailored exactly to his needs, and in time I saw how short-sighted I'd been. I had wanted my husband to become a Christian for my convenience. God loved him for his eternal destiny. Where I had been impatient for a quick fix, God knew a complete remodelling of our marriage would be needed. He had to bulldoze my old attitudes so that he might help us rebuild on his sure foundation. When hope fades, he is the only third person in a marriage who can make it work.'

> ***'If you remain in me and my words remain in you, ask whatever you wish, and it will be given you.'***
>
> *John 15:7*

Virginia Baty was to learn that God not only heals our diseases but also heals from sin and its consequences.

'It was January 1978, and the year had begun pretty much like any other. However, three weeks into the month, I discovered a lump in one breast. My first response was denial, but troubled thoughts ran through my mind: It was not cancer – it just couldn't be cancer; there's no cancer in my family. I couldn't even tell my husband. With much fear and trembling, I could hardly get through my days. Finally, I had to tell him, and he immediately insisted that I make an appointment with the doctor. I still rejected the idea that cancer was a possibility – there had to be some mistake.

'The gynaecologist confirmed there was a suspicious lump, most likely a tumour. Even though it could be benign, I should see a surgeon as soon as possible.

'Following x-rays, we discussed my situation and options. There was a tumour and the doctor wanted me to have surgery right away. I was still sure it couldn't be anything, and I knew a biopsy would prove that. I even asked for a week's reprieve since we had already planned a trip for the upcoming weekend to see some of our family 200 miles away. The doctor reluctantly gave permission but insisted on scheduling the surgery for the following week.

'We went on our trip but the words that we had just heard weren't far from our minds the entire time. We told our loved ones and friends, who all began to pray for me. Without the knowledge of this prayer support, I am not sure I could have carried on during the next few days and weeks. Even as I signed the papers prior to surgery, there was no doubt in my mind that I would be OK. My surgeon was a Christian and he prayed for me before I was taken into surgery, which was a real comfort. Oh, yes, I was somewhat fearful, but with my husband standing by, I went to sleep fully trusting that God would take care of me.

Surgery took six hours and a tumour the size of an egg was removed, along with twenty-four infected lymph nodes and leaders, spreading under the breastbone. It *was* cancer! The doctor indicated he didn't know if they had removed all of the infected tissue during the radical mastectomy. They even had to do a skin graft from my leg to the chest wall. We were told chemotherapy treatments would follow my recovery from surgery.

'It's at times like this that you realise only the prayers of God's people can and will help to carry you through. *"Therefore confess your sins to each other and pray for each other so that you may be healed. The prayer of a righteous man is powerful and effective"* (James 5:16).

'It took me four months to recover from the surgery. During that time, as I waited for chemotherapy to begin, I became very apprehensive. The devil taunted me with fears, and I was quite unsettled. You know how the enemy works, "You would not be fearful if you really were a Christian." "Where is your faith, Virginia?" Finally, after much prayer and counsel, I came to realise that my fears were only human and it was OK. God would see me through.

'I literally fed on God's Word. *"Fear not, for I have redeemed you; I have summoned you by name; you are mine. When you pass through the waters, I will be with you; and when you pass through the rivers, they will not sweep over you. When you walk through the fire, you will not be burned; the flames will not set you ablaze"* (Isaiah 43:1, 2).

'Another scripture that encouraged me greatly was, *"So do not fear, for I am with you; do not be dismayed, for I am your God. I will strengthen you and help you; I will uphold you with my righteous right hand'* (Isaiah 41:10).

'I underwent twelve months of chemotherapy treatments and had very little of the severe side-effects that many experience. I was even able to work part-time that year. God drew very close to me through my reading of his Word and meditating on it.

'During my hospitalisation, our youngest son, who was deep into a life of drugs, alcohol, and waywardness, was broken-hearted about my illness. He kept telling me that he was the one who should be suffering – he was the one who had done wrong; why was I suffering? We encouraged him to understand that trouble comes to the just and unjust alike. We continued to pray, and as the time went on we began to see a change in his attitude, and finally he did make a decision to give his life to Christ. I truly believe my bout with cancer was used by God to help bring him to the Saviour. Of course there were other people and situations that affected his decision, but my son has now been a Christian for eighteen years. Praise the Lord!'

God not only heals our diseases, but more importantly he heals from sin and its consequences as well. God's healing through Virginia confirms that the challenges we go through are often just the experiences that give others the courage to go on.

'Praise be to the God and Father of our Lord Jesus Christ, the Father of compassion and the God of all comfort, who comforts us in all our troubles, so that we can comfort those in any trouble with the comfort we ourselves have received from God.'

2 Corinthians 1:3, 4

Chapter 12

He's able

'Now unto him that is able to keep you from falling, and to present you faultless before the presence of his glory with exceeding joy.'

Jude 24, KJV

'If I only touch his cloak, I will be healed' (Matt 9:21). It was a poor women who spoke these words – a women who for twelve years had suffered from a disease that made her life a burden. She had spent all her means on the remedies of her day, only to be told that her illness was incurable. But she had heard of the Great Teacher who was able to heal.

As Jesus was making his way near to where the afflicted woman was standing, all she knew was that she had to get near to him. No doubt many times in the past she had tried, but in vain; this might be her last opportunity. Even so, she dared not talk to him or even stop the procession. Her only thought was, "If I can just touch just the hem of his garment." And that one touch proved to be the source of healing, for "immediately" she was healed. It had been the touch of faith.

Jan Clark's experience is a modern day example of the way that fervent prayer can move the hands of God.

A plaque hangs in Dr Perry's obstetrics/gynaecological (O/B) office. There is a photograph of a beautiful mother frolicking on a sandy beach with a little baby. Above the picture is the following inscription:

'On March 13th a year ago, God saved my life. It's true.
For all your prayers and acts of kindness,
I want to show appreciation to you.
The power of prayer is miraculous; this I learned first-hand.
The true meaning of love and friendship I now also understand.
"He is able" is the song that still rings in my ears.
I know it is God's love that will carry me through the years.
"This sickness will not end in death, it's to glorify God's name"
Is a special verse given to my family that now as my own I claim
So thank you so much for all you did to help pull me through.
My family and I are truly blessed to have friends as dear as you!

Janet Cason Clark, March 1997'

An O/B patient asks a nurse to tell her the story behind the plaque, and the nurse sits down and smiles as she begins to share. It was given to Dr Perry on the first anniversary of Jan's miraculous healing. This is Jan's story.

'On 12 March 1996 Jan had lunch with her sister Jill. They were both excited about the upcoming birth of Jan's baby, and, in fact, Jan had to leave right after lunch in order to keep her 1.45pm appointment with her O/B physician. This was to be the first baby for Jan and her husband Greg. Her expected date of delivery was confirmed by ultrasound to be 15 April.

'There were no complications during the pregnancy until that day. During the office visit, Jan's blood pressure was noted to be high. Her diastolic blood pressure was noted to be at 90. Jan was sent directly to Labour and Delivery (L&D) for more accurate monitoring.

'When she was admitted to the Delivery Unit, Jan's blood pressure was monitored. All tests appeared reassuring. Pregnancy-induced hypertension was the diagnosis. Late in the afternoon Jan and Greg were allowed to go home. She was directed to remain on absolute bed rest for the weekend.

'In the early evening, Jan started feeling pain in the upper right side of her body. Greg rushed her back to the hospital. She was admitted again to L&D. Her diastolic blood pressure was 90, and her physician began to treat the blood pressure with magnesium sulphate, which will usually bring down the blood pressure. He also wanted to review everything with new lab. work, early the next morning. Depending on her condition, he would either induce labour or perform a Caesarean (C) -section.

'Over the next two hours, the blood pressure elevated to 140/100-110, normal being 120/80, and Jan continued to complain of severe epigastric pain. The decision was made to perform an emergency C-section.

'At 2:27am Addison Thomas Clark was delivered. Greg and Jan had a beautiful baby boy. Showing them the abnormal placenta, the O/B physician said, "If Jan had in fact carried to forty weeks, Addison would have died. He was not receiving enough nourishment from his mother's body." This was one of many wondrous miracles! God had spared Addison's life, bringing to remembrance a song Jan had sung:

He's able, he's able,
I know he's able, I know my Lord
Is able to carry me through!

'Jan would sometimes substitute the word "us" for "me". She would sing the words to the precious baby in her womb, "Yes, Lord you are able to carry us through!" It was always a sweet, tender moment between Jan and Addison, "God is able to carry us through this pregnancy."

'The Lord did carry Addison through. The baby was taken to the Neonatal Intensive Care Unit (NICU) for observation because he was only 4 pounds 15 ounces and premature. Because the pain continued in the upper right side of her body and her blood pressure remained high, Jan was kept in Delivery, but after a few hours she was rolled in the hospital bed into the NICU to see Addison. She and Greg stayed and visited with him for thirty minutes. How excited they were to have their first baby! They were such proud parents.

After the baby had been moved to the Well Baby Nursery, Greg asked that Addison could be taken to Jan for his 9am feed. As he started to breast feed, being proud new parents, they were filled with joy and excitement. They had such a wonderful family time together. Then, after an hour of visitation, Addison was taken back to the Nursery. Life was wonderful. God is so good!

'Later that morning, a maternity nurse came in to give Jan her medications. She was complaining of progressively severe pain in her right upper side, but suddenly she experienced a reduction in her pain and told the nurse, "I feel better, and the pain is not there." The nurse discovered Jan's blood pressure had dropped dangerously low. It was now 70/40. Her condition was deteriorating rapidly.

'The medical team rushed into the room. They worked fast with rapid efficiency. Arterial lines and central venous necklines were inserted. IV fluids were increased. Jan's blood count was quickly found to be extremely low. She was losing blood! She had an internal haemorrhage. Whole blood was administered, but Jan's condition continued to deteriorate until she was in profound shock. A decision was made to perform an exploratory surgery with the likely probability of finding a rupture of the liver.

'As Jan was being rushed into surgery, Greg was standing against the wall of the hallway. He could hear Jan softly singing, "I don't ever have to be afraid, Jesus takes care of me."

'She called back to Greg, "Raise my son as a Christian!" This could have been their last goodbye. Greg did not know if he would ever see his wife alive again. With tears streaming down his face, he saw the surgeon running down the hall, taking off his jacket. The physician explained to Greg and the family that he had never seen anything like this before. She was in a grave condition.

'Having told the family of the situation, the nurse set up a room across the hall for them. In the little room, the devoted, praying family went down on their knees, pleading that God would spare Jan's life. They sent out prayer requests all over to other family members and friends. Intercession of the saints began to go up to the throne of God, pleading for Jan's life.

'During surgery it was seen that there was a massive rupture of the capsule of the liver extending through the entire right lobe. The liver has a thin coating like "saran wrap". If the liver becomes too engorged by the HELLP syndrome, which Jan was suffering from, it will literally burst, and that's what happened to Jan's liver. The bleeding was slowed as, for over an hour, the surgeon applied pressure by placing his hand directly on Jan's liver to stop the bleeding.

'Jan received eighteen units of blood and blood products. Surgical packing, to stop the severe bleeding, was then placed all around the liver, and small drainage tubes were inserted from the liver area to the stomach. The incision was closed with the cloth packing inside. There was nothing else to do. Jan was transferred to the Surgical Intensive Care Unit, and placed on a ventilator. There, Greg and the family had a conference with the surgeons, who explained that the sub-capsulary layer of the liver had ruptured from the most severe case of toxaemia and PIH (Pregnancy Induced Hypertension) that they had ever seen through years of surgery and deliveries. While toxaemia is often seen during pregnancy, the physicians said that liver rupture was rare and explained that the packing would have to be removed in twenty-four hours to prevent overwhelming infection. Now Jan was facing yet another surgery, the third in two days. They would not know her prognosis until forty-eight hours from the time the packing was removed.

'Removing the packing was extremely dangerous since bleeding could recur. Jan's sister Jill asked the surgeon, "What happens if it still bleeds?" The surgeon replied, "I don't know, but what can I do? There is also a high risk of damage to her lungs, kidney, and heart, because she's lost so much blood." The final consensus of the surgeons was, "We're doing everything that can be done medically, but we need someone else to take care of this. She is not out of the woods yet."

'The prayers of the saints were bombarding the gates of heaven. Jan and Greg needed a miracle. Then their prayers began to be answered. While Dr Perry, Jan's gynaecologist, was walking down the hospital hallway, silently petitioning the throne of heaven to spare Jan's life, he felt that God spoke to his heart. He felt impressed that Jan would not die.

'Sitting in the lobby, Jan's mother and sister saw Dr Perry, so they asked him, "Do you think she is going to be OK?" Dr Perry felt able to tell them, "I think the Lord has assured me that Jan is going to be OK."

'These words brought the first bit of comfort to a family in distress. They knew the Lord was able to spare Jan, but what was his will for her life? Respecting the sovereignty of the Lord, they pondered these words in their hearts, while at the same time, to hear the surgeon's words had brought such peace and comfort to them.

'For only a few minutes at a time, each member of the family was allowed to visit Jan. The ventilator was loud and noisy, and her body was swollen beyond recognition. Jan was so lifeless, her colouring a greyish white. So white! It was a shock to the family to see her in this condition. She had always been so vibrant, so full of life. They had never before experienced a health crisis in the family, and now it almost took their breath away to see their beloved wife, sister, and daughter in such a grave state. It was a test of anyone's faith. For Greg and the family, it was going to be a long night. They had to trust God.

'Continuing with the prayer vigil, Greg and the family prayed. Jan's mother said, "I'm going to wrestle with God all night just like Jacob. I'm going to keep praying until I know the Lord has heard me." During the night they would take turns to pray, and continued to plead with God to let Jan live. Their church pastor gave the Scripture verse John 11:4 to Jan's mother: *"This sickness will not end in death. No, it is for God's glory so that God's Son may be glorified through it."*

'For the second time, a word of comfort had come to them. Jan will live! Hope began to spring in their hearts. Even in the hospital, word swept quickly about Jan Clark. She had worked as a nurse in the Well Baby Nursery for ten years. There is something about hearing of a new mother fighting for, and possibly losing, her life in childbirth that makes for a "silence". It is usually a time of great joy. To hear of a new father making funeral plans for his wife pricks at the core of even the hardest of hearts. Also, she was one of their very own. Employees were praying for Jan, even people she did not know very well. They would come to Greg and the family and tell them, "We are praying."

'Usually the hospital is a noisy, bustling place, but Jan was on the hearts and minds of the entire staff, and there was a silence in the hospital, a heaviness in the air.

'Meanwhile, Greg had a ten-foot banner made for Jan. He hung it up on the wall opposite her hospital bed. The inscription read, "HE'S ABLE". He wanted Jan to remember the song she had sung to Addison every day before he was born.

'Being a nurse, Jan knew she was in serious trouble when she was told she would have to go back into surgery. She was disheartened, but remembering the words to the song she said, "Yes, Lord, you are able to carry me through to live to take care of my son."

'At around 1pm Jan was taken back into surgery. As she was wheeled into the operating room (OR), there stood Dr Perry. He told her, "I'm going to pray for you during your surgery." Clasping her hand to comfort her, he whispered into her ear as the anaesthesia was administered, "Jesus is here with you; don't be afraid."

'The surgeons had to remove the packing to see if the liver would bleed again. With the OR filled with surgeons and support staff, Dr Perry prayed as each of the packs was carefully removed. There was only a slight oozing of blood, and with the removal of each layer, Dr Perry would quietly say, "Thank you, Lord." The haemorrhaging had stopped. The surgeons were encouraged.

'While Jan was in surgery, Greg and the family went into the hospital chapel. There they continued to pray and plead for the Lord to save Jan's life. After the surgery, the surgeons counselled with the family. "If we could go twenty-four to forty-eight hours without major complications, we would feel a lot better about things. She is still not quite out of the woods yet." Dr Perry told the family, "I never felt the power of God more than in that operating room." Jan was taken back to the SICU, still on the ventilator.

'In the SICU, one of Dr Perry's nurses, who had befriended Jan, came to visit her, pinning a little gold angel on her hospital gown. Jan would reach up and touch the angel for encouragement. When Dr Perry came by to visit Jan, she gestured with her hand, and blew him a kiss, as her way of thanking him.

'When Greg came back from the nursery to spend time with Jan, she would write out instructions regarding Addison, such as, "Sing and have worship with Addison." Jill would go down to the Well Baby Nursery, and tenderly hold Addison in her arms, gently rocking him and singing to him.

'While lying in her bed, Jan could see the banner, "He's able!", and she would remember the words of the song. On the ventilator, Jan could not speak out loud, but would silently sing these words in her heart, adding, "Lord, you are able to carry me through to live to take care of my son." Then the forty-eight-hour critical period was over and Jan was still alive! She did not experience any more major complications. Her heart had not failed. Her kidneys had not failed. Her lungs had not failed. The surgeons told Greg and the family, " Jan is out of the woods." She was taken off the ventilator. It was as if the Lord answered the prayers of his people, according to Ezekiel 16:6: *"Then I passed by and saw you kicking about in your blood, and as you lay there in your blood I said to you, 'Live!' "*

'He was able to carry Jan through from death to take care of her son, Addison. Greg and the family rejoiced. He is able!

'Over the next week Jan's condition continued to improve. During that time she received more units of red blood cells. Her blood pressure remained stable. Two weeks later Jan, still weak but feeling better, was discharged home. The Lord had saved her life. The Lord had in fact carried her through the very shadow of death. A ruptured liver along with pregnancy has a fatality rate of well over 80%.

'One year later, on the anniversary of 13 March, Jan and Greg dedicated 'their' room in the SICU. During the dedication ceremony, most of the physicians and staff gathered with Greg and Jan to remember the marvellous healing God had performed. On the wall is an inscription, which reads, not surprisingly, ***"He's able"***.

'Jan wanted the story never to be forgotten. When other people's loved ones were lying in the same SICU room, in the same SICU bed, she wanted families to be able to open the Word of God and read Psalm 56:13: *"For you have delivered me from death and my feet from stumbling, that I may walk before God in the light of life."*

'Today, Jan and Greg are raising their 3-year-old Addison. And on Jan's car licence plate is the inscription, "GODS ABL", declaring to the world, "**He's able to carry me through!**"

The nurse finished telling the story. Smiling, the new patient said, 'He's able to carry me through, too!' Patting her stomach, she walked into the examination room for her doctor's visit, all the while telling her unborn child a message that applies to us all: "This same God is able to carry you through."

ONE Appendix

Biblical promises of healing

'"But I will restore you to health and heal your wounds," declares the Lord.' Jeremiah 30:17

'"This is what the Lord, the God of your father David, says: I have heard your prayer and seen your tears; I will heal you."' 2 Kings 20:5

'"If my people, who are called by my name, will humble themselves and pray and seek my face and turn from their wicked ways, then will I hear from heaven and will forgive their sin and will heal their land."' 2 Chronicles 7:14

'Be merciful to me, Lord, for I am faint; O Lord, heal me, for my bones are in agony.' Psalm 6:2

'Heal me, O Lord, and I shall be healed; save me and I shall be saved, for you are the one I praise.' Jeremiah 17:14

'Jesus said to Jairus, "Don't be afraid; just believe, and she will be healed."' Luke 8:50

'Dear friend, I pray that you may enjoy good health and that all may go well with you, even as your soul is getting along well.' 3 John 2

'He heals the broken hearted and binds up their wounds.' Psalm 147:3

'The Lord is close to the brokenhearted and saves those who are crushed in spirit. A righteous man may have many troubles, but the Lord delivers him from them all.' Psalm 34:18, 19

Appendix ONE

'Do you not know? Have you not heard? The Lord is the everlasting God, the Creator of the ends of the earth. He will not grow tired or weary, and his understanding no-one can fathom. He gives strength to the weary and increases the power of the weak. Even youths grow tired and weary, and young men stumble and fall; but those who hope in the Lord will renew their strength. They will soar on wings like eagles; they will run and not grow weary, they will walk and not be faint.' Isaiah 40:28-31

'My flesh and my heart may fail, but God is the strength of my heart and my portion for ever.' Psalm 73:26

'I am bowed down and brought very low; all day long I go about mourning. My back is filled with searing pain; there is no health in my body. I am feeble and utterly crushed; I groan in anguish of heart. All my longings lie open before you, O Lord; my sighing is not hidden from you. My heart pounds, my strength fails me; even the light has gone from my eyes. My friends and companions avoid me because of my wounds; my neighbours stay far away. Those who seek my life set their traps, those who would harm me talk of my ruin; all day long they plot deception. I am like a deaf man, who cannot hear, like a mute, who cannot open his mouth; I have become like a man who does not hear, whose mouth can offer no reply. I wait for you, O Lord; you will answer, O Lord my God.' Psalm 38:6-15

'Look to the Lord and his strength; seek his face always. Remember the wonders he has done, his miracles, and the judgments he pronounced.' Psalm 105:4, 5

'You guide me with your counsel, and afterwards you will take me into glory. Whom have I in heaven but you? And earth has nothing I desire besides you. My flesh and my heart may fail, but God is the strength of my heart and my portion for ever.' Psalm 73:24-26

' "For how can this servant of my lord talk with you, my lord? As for me, no strength remains in me now, nor is any breath left in me." Then again, the one having the likeness of a man touched me and strengthened me. And he said, "O man greatly beloved, fear not! Peace be to you; be strong, yes, be strong!" ' Daniel 10:17-19, NKJV

'Strengthen the feeble hands, steady the knees that give way; say to those with fearful hearts, "Be strong, do not fear; your God will come, he will come with vengeance; with divine retribution he will come to save you." Then will the eyes of the blind be opened and the ears of the deaf un-stopped. Then will the lame leap like a deer, and the mute tongue shout for joy. Water will gush forth in the wilderness and streams in the desert. The burning sand will become a pool, the thirsty ground bubbling springs.'
Isaiah 35:3-7

' "So do not fear, for I am with you; do not be dismayed, for I am your God. I will strengthen you and help you; I will uphold you with my righteous right hand." ' Isaiah 41:10

' "As a shepherd looks after his scattered flock when he is with them, so will I look after my sheep. I will rescue them from all the places where they were scattered on a day of clouds and darkness . . . . I will search for the lost and bring back the strays. I will bind up the injured and strengthen the weak." ' Ezekiel 34:12, 16

'O Lord my God, I called to you for help and you healed

me. O Lord, you brought me up from the grave; you spared me from going down into the pit.' Psalm 30:2, 3

'Weeping may remain for a night, but rejoicing comes in the morning.' Psalm 30:5

'But he was pierced for our transgressions; he was crushed for our iniquities; the punishment that brought us peace was upon him, and by his wounds we are healed.'
Isaiah 53:5

'I am under vows to you, O God; I will present my thank offerings to you. For you have delivered me from death and my feet from stumbling, that I may walk before God in the light of life.' Psalm 56:12, 13

'Is any one of you sick? He should call the elders of the church to pray over him and anoint him with oil in the name of the Lord. And the prayer offered in faith will make the sick person well; the Lord will raise him up. If he has sinned, he will be forgiven . . . . The prayer of a righteous man is powerful and effective.' James 5:14-16

'If we are distressed, it is for your comfort and salvation; if we are comforted, it is for your comfort, which produces in you patient endurance of the same sufferings we suffer.' 2 Corinthians 1:6

'Worship the Lord your God, and his blessing will be on your food and water. I will take away sickness from among you.' Exodus 23:25

Appendix TWO

Scriptural passages of people healed

Passage	Description
Genesis 20:17	Abimelech
Exodus 4:6, 7	Moses' hand
Numbers 12:1-14	Miriam's leprosy
16:41-50	Plague on Israelites
21:4-9	Israelites bitten by snakes
1 Samuel 16:14-23	Saul's tormented spirit
1 Kings 13:4-6	King Jeroboam's arm
17:17-24	Widow of Zarephath's son
2 Kings 4:8-37	Shunammite's son
5:1-14	Naaman's leprosy
20:1-11	Hezekiah's illness
Job, chapters 1-42	Job
Matthew	
4:23	Multitudes
8:2-4	Leprosy
8:5-13	Centurion's servant
8:14, 15	Peter's mother-in-law
8:16, 17	Multitudes and demon-possessed
8:28-34	Demoniac
9:2-8	Paralysed man
9:18, 19, 23-26	Jairus's daugher
9:20-22	Woman with bleeding
9:27-31	Two blind men
9:32, 33	Dumb demoniac
9:35; 11:4, 5	Multitudes
12:22	Blind and dumb demoniac
14:14; 14:34-36;	

15:30; 19:2	Multitudes
15:21-28	Canaanite woman's daughter
17:14-18	Child with evil spirit
20:29-34	Two blind men
21:14	Blind and lame in temple
Mark	
1:21-28	Man with unclean spirit
7:31-37	Deaf and dumb man
8:22-26	Blind man
Luke	
1:18-21, 62-64	Zechariah's dumbness
5:15	Multitudes
7:11-17	Widow of Nain's son raised
8:2	Mary Magdalene cleansed
13:10-13	Crippled woman
14:1-4	Man with dropsy
17:11-19	Ten men with leprosy
22:50, 51	Malchus's ear
John	
4:46-53	Nobleman's son
5:1-9	Impotent man
9:1-11	Man born blind
11:1-44	Lazarus raised
Acts	
3:1-7	Lame beggar
9:32-35	Aeneas at Lydda
9:36-43	Dorcas at Joppa
14:8-10	Lame man at Lystra
14:19, 20	Paul, after stoning
20:7-12	Eutychus from dead
28:7-9	Publius's father in Malta, with others.

Notes

Notes